To:

aSTIGMAtism In My Soul!

A Black American Males adventure from dead broke to millionaire to dead broke to "white collar crime" incarceration in the United States Federal Bureau of Prisons (The Feds) to back on top!

volume III

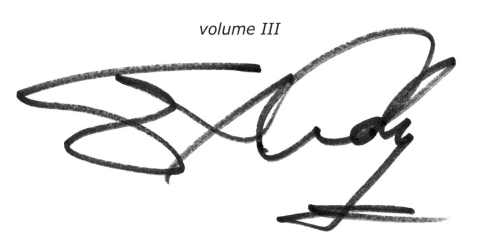

ISBN: 978-0-578-96873-5

DEDICATION

GEORGIA GUNBY

This book is dedicated to my mother, Georgia Gunby, who recently passed away in October 2020. Who has/had taught me so much of what I know that has contributed to my success. Who mentored me even when we fought and disagreed. Who showed me what "hard work" was and how it benefits our lives and souls. Who showed me how to bounce back from mistakes, setbacks and failures and "do it right" the next time. Who showed me how to go from picking cotton for $.75 cents a day as a child in Lincolnton, Georgia to becoming a Registered Nurse in the New York City Metropolitan Area (North Jersey), buying her own home and rental properties to pay for her lifestyle. Who taught me to take no shit from anybody and to always speak my heart and mind. Who loved my SUN, Lil Sean, in a genuine, sincere and true way that only true love can be expressed.

I love you Ma. I miss you Ma. And I'mma take care of Lil Sean and give him everything you wanted to give him.

I GOT IT!!

Your son,

Sean

ABOUT THE AUTHOR

Sean Xavier Gunby, Sr. was born in Passaic, New Jersey and raised in Clifton, New Jersey. He has lived in Atlanta, Georgia, and other towns and cities in North Jersey.

Sean has a Bachelor of Science degree in Accounting from Morris Brown College *(a Historically Black College & University located in Atlanta, GA).*

Sean earned his Master of Science degree in Financial Management from the New Jersey Institute of Technology in Newark, New Jersey where he graduated Cum Laude.

Sean earned his Ph.D., Doctorate degree in The Feds at Federal Correctional Institution at Morgantown in Morgantown, West Virginia.

Sean is a professional golf caddie.

Sean has worked in the corporate world as a Financial Analyst doing mergers & acquisitions of real estate brokerage companies throughout the United States. As a Financial Analyst, Sean played a major role in the analysis and acquisition of over 100 real estate brokerage companies throughout the United States of America with an annual Sales Volume of over $10 Billion dollars.

Sean has taught as an Adjunct Professor of Pre-Algebra at Passaic County Community College in Paterson, NJ, Bergen County Community College in Paramus, NJ and Essex County College in Newark, NJ.

He was a licensed New Jersey Real Estate Broker and operated a successful realty brokerage, tax preparation and consulting business with over 1,300 clients in 17 different states until he allowed greed to infect his spirit and mind which lead to him being indicted and pleading guilty to getting his clients back bigger refunds than they were entitled to by overstating deductions and credits. These were federal charges and resulted in Sean serving 15 months, 15 days and 19 hours in The United States Federal Bureau of Prisons or "The Feds".

Sean remains an expert real estate investor.

Sean is an experienced stock and options trader and trades his own account.

Today, Sean is a published author and lives in North Jersey, owns and operates a successful window cleaning business and is a Professional Black Father of a Black Sun.

THE IMPETUS FOR WRITING THIS LITERARY DOCUMENT

This document is the follow-up and continuation of **aSTIGMAtism In My Soul – Volume II**, and the last book of the **aSTIGMAtism In My Soul** trilogy series. I am so proud of myself that I have saw this project all the way through to it's completion and kept my word to myself that I was going to write these books, tell my story and control my narrative.

Finishing this book adds to my already high SELF-CONFIDENCE and lets me know definitively that I can write more books.

Hence,

aSTIGMAtism In My Soul – Volume III

THE REST OF THIS PAGE INTENTIONALLY LEFT BLANK

A NOTE FROM THE AUTHOR

I would like to thank everyone who has supported my work and other platforms. You have touched me in so many different ways that I can't even begin to enumerate.

This document was not proof-read, checked for spelling, perused for typos or edited by anyone but me. I did not edit this document at all. What I wrote the first time is what got printed. How can I edit my SOUL?

Thank you

Sean G

THE REST OF THIS PAGE INTENTIONALLY LEFT BLANK

Monday, April 30, 2018

Here we are. I am shining brighter than ever. Goals are being reached and achieved at a consistent pace. My focus is still clear and the clarity with which I envision my life is as translucent at oxygen or air. I am determined to find a glorious end to my journey here on Earth.

Finished up my window cleaning route today early, did some calisthetics workout in the park, just took me a shower and getting ready to go pick Lil Sean up from school as he has a baseball game tonight at 5:30.

I am in absolute tremendous spiritual, mental and physical shape and condition and don't see anything hindering my progress. My success is assured.

My life is the shit!!

I fuckin' love being me!!

Thursday, May 3, 2018

Under no circumstances can you quit going after your goals. No matter how fuckin' hard it gets, how many times you fail trying to get there, no matter how many naysayers and haters you have rooting against you…. YOU CAN'T FUCKIN' QUIT!! It ain't for them … It's for you! This is your life, your chance, your opportunity, your vision, your passion, your dream…… Go get the muthaphucka!!!

Peace Out!

Wednesday, May 09, 2018

Things are progressing…albeit… one-inch-at-a-time, nonetheless, they are progressing.

The day today was success. Got Lil Sean showered and dressed for school. Cooked him some pancakes and eggs. Played catch with the football before school in the parking lot. Dropped him off to school. Completed my window cleaning route for the day. Filmed a video for my YouTube Channel. Did some homework (updated my stock market charts that I'm keeping by hand). Now I'm writing on my book. Following my agenda. Practicing self-discipline and executing my plan.

Reconnected with an old friend from college today via Facebook, she called and we spoke for 82 minutes straight, reminiscing about days past, catching up on days present and articulating our days that are in-front of us. It is true that 'seeing and talking to old friends is good for the soul".

Wow!! I'm 49 years old. Got some bumps and bruises on my spirit but I'm still here, shinin' looking and feeling better than ever. I love my life where it is and where I am going. My best days are still in front of me. I have never felt this good ever at any point in my life. I'm self-directed, focused, determined, disciplined and impervious to external influence. My shit is hermetic…..."air tight".

I fully understand in the entire sense of the thought that …"out life experiences shape us and make us who we are and without them we would not be who we are today."…. That shit is REAL! I don't regret anything.. instead… I embrace everything.

It's good to be me!

Thursday, May 24, 2018

Happy Birthday to My Sun, Sean X. Gunby, Jr. Turned 7 years old today. Wow!! The best thing that has every happened in my life. I resurrected myself through the birth of my child; my cipher is complete. Gonna take him and some of the kids from the neighborhood bowling Saturday and get them some pizza.

On my was to speak to some high school Jr's and Sr's at Eastside High School in Newark, NJ this morning. This is my first public speaking engagement and I'm excited. I'm going to put it down.

This book is taking me places and introducing me to people that I never would have gone or me had it not been for this book. It has taken on a life of its own and is propelling me forward to where I want to go and where I belong.

ngs are progressing...albeit... one-inch-at-a-time, nonetheless, they are progressing.

My 1st Sojourn To Africa

I will never forget this trip ever. When I had my tax practice in full swing, after every tax season I would take a trip/vacation as a reward to myself for having completed another stressful-ass tax season.

In 2007, I went to my 20-year high school class reunion and was speaking to one of my classmates who told me that she had just came back from a trip to Egypt. I asked her for the particulars and how she managed the trip. She told that she went through a travel agency called Gate1 Travel and that if I went online everything would be there as to how to go and that it was super easy to set up at a cost of about $2,500 for a 14 night/15 day tour which included air fare, hotel accommodations, food, 7 day cruise down The Nile River including the cabin on the cruise ship, food, air fare within Egypt, tickets into the Cairo Museum, Pyramids and other temples, plus travel by bus within Egypt.

I went home the same muthaphuckin' night and booked my trip. This was in 2008. I was so excited and filled all the way up with anticipation. I couldn't fuckin' wait. *"Oh shit... I'm going to Africa....I'm going to Egypt... I'm going to see The Pyramids... I'm going to go on a cruise down The Nile.... Oh shit.... Can't fuckin' believe this shit...."*

My tax season ended April 16th, 2008 and 30 days later I was on my way "home" to Africa, "The Mother Land" for the 1st time in my life.

The days leading up to my departure for Egypt were filled with excitement, anticipation, anxiety and my fuckin' horrible allergies. At this time in my life my physical fitness was below average, I was fat and on the verge of being obese so my allergies would really bother me big time and if I wasn't careful they would turn into a full blown flu. Well this is exactly what happened. The few days leading up to my leaving my allergies started to kick up and I began to fight them with over-the-counter allergy medication like Benadryl, etc. To no avail, my allergies morphed into a full-blown flu.

Well the day finally came for me to leave. I remember getting car service from my office to Kennedy Airport in Queens, NY and feeling like I was embarking on the UNKNOWN and feeling excited about it. I boarded the plane, we pushed back from the gate, taxi'd down the runway and took off head to Africa. My allergies in full bloom. I'm sneezing, nose running, eyes red and watering just all fucked up. I'm medicating with the intention of eradicating this minor inconvenience before we land or that perhaps when I get to Africa, Egypt, the new climate and atmosphere will help make the allergies go away.

WRONG!!!

11 hours later, when we landed in Cairo, Egypt my allergies had worsened and was definitely going to turn into a full-blown flu. SHIT!! GOD DAMN!!! MUTHAPHUCKA!! I don't believe this shit! My first trip to Africa and I get sick coming over here…. DAMN!! Well fuck it, I'll just make the best of it was my thought process. I didn't come this far to not see the pyramids. I toughed it out.

I will never forget this for as long as I live. When we landed at the Cairo Airport and deplaned, we did not deplane into a tunnel that leads you into the airport like here in America, we deplaned directly onto the tarmac of the airport. Egypt Air had a grounds crew position of huge set of steps next to the exit of the plane and we walked down the stairs directly onto the ground. Even though my allergies were weighing on me, I was super excited about having landed, exhausted from the 11-hour plane ride, fucked up from my allergies and totally anxious about seeing The Pyramids. I got my back pack, put it on, and walked toward the exit of the aircraft. When it came time for me to "actually and physically" exit the aircraft, I stepped out of the plane onto the stairs and I remember that when I took my 1st breathe of that African, Egyptian, "oxygen, air and atmosphere", the feeling that I got that went through my entire body, mind and soul was "that I was not in a foreign and strange place". It was as if my soul knew that it belonged right where it was. It was as if I was truly "at home".

I felt more at peace and "at home" right there on that airport tarmac that I had ever felt in North Jersey where I was born and raised. It was an epiphany and a spiritual experience unlike any other I had experienced up until that point in my life. From that moment I was never the same ever again in my life. This moment changed the way I looked at myself, the way I looked at the world and the very essence of who I was going forward. I have never been the same since that moment. It's a moment I will never forget. I have been back to Africa several times subsequent to this day and have never experienced that feeling ever again.

The first 3 – 4 days we moved around in Cairo, visited the Sphinx, The Pyramids, the Cairo Museum and saw some other sites. My first site of The Pyramids was from a distance as we drove on the tour bus from the airport toward the hotel. I saw 2 of the 3 (The Great Pyramid and the middle one) and it sent my mind and soul into flight. *Ohhh shit… I'm here… I can see them muthaphuckas right dere!!! Ohhh shit!! Can't wait until tomorrow for us to actually go to the Giza Plateau so I can see them up close.*

Seeing The Pyramids for first time was "life changing". I touched them, climbed them, sat on them, walked on them and stared at them for hours we stayed there. Some of the base blocks of limestone that served at "above the ground foundation" for The Pyramids were the size of a Toyota Corolla. 10 tons, 15 tons, 20 ton blocks "each" (1 block) of limestone that had been quarried at a limestone quarry 12 -15 miles away and transported to The Giza Plateau with a mathematical ingenuity beyond human comprehension. This was one of the most amazing things I had ever seen in my life. I took it all in and just let it marinate for the remainder of the time there on The Giza Plateau and my sojourn in Egypt.

SHIT!!!! MUTHAPHUCKA!!!

I'm sick as a muthaphucka now. Full Blown FLU! DAMN!! Don't believe this shit. I fight. I fight. I fight. I buy over-the-counter flu and cold medications in the drugstores in Egypt. I drink tea with lemon and honey. To no avail .. I'm fucked up and sick as a muthaphucka in Africa/Egypt, 11 hours from Jersey City, 11 hours from Walgreens, CVS or Rite Aid, I don't speak the language, I'm with a bunch of strangers in my tour group.. unfuckin-believable!! I'm already physically weak from the flu and now I'm starting to get mentally weak with negative thoughts. What am I going to do? This is Day #2 and I'm here for 15 days. How am I going to make it? What am I gonna do?

I tell my lead tour guide (I forget her name but she was the most gracious and best tour guide I've ever had on any of my over seas trips) that if I don't start feeling better by tomorrow (Day #3) that I'm cancelling my tour/trip and I'm going to the airport and coming back to the United States. She told me *"No Sean... just hold off... we leave for Luxor tomorrow and I will call a doctor to come meet us on the cruise ship and he will have some medicine for you."* I said ok. The next day we flew from Cairo to Luxor and I was worse and getting even worse as the time went on. We landed at the airport, got on the tour bus that took us to the cruise ship and we made our way to the cruise ship.

Once we got to the cruise ship I went to the tour guide and she called the doctor. I went and laid down in my cabin and waited for the doctor to show up. I was sick as hell. A little while later I heard a knock at my door. I get up and open the door and there is an Egyptian man standing there with a faded t-shirt, worn out jean, flip flops and a medicine bag... he says "I'm the doctor"...

Aahhhhhh man!!! I'm like no fuckin' way man! (to myself). This muthaphucka is the doctor... I'm gonna die over here in Africa. I let him into my cabin and he starts asking me the familiar doctor questions (do you have a fever, how do you feel? What's wrong?). I explain to him what's up and he looks at me and says he wants to give me a shot. I ask, "with a needle?". He says "Yes".. I say "What kind of shot? A shot of what? When? Right now?". He says, "some penicillin and yes right now".

I said "AAAAHHHHHHHH SHIT!!! A muthphuckin doctor with a t-shirt, worn out jeans and flip flops wants to stick in needle in my body right here in the cruise ship cabin, in Africa/Egypt, 11 hours from the United States and Jersey City.... Holy shit!!!!!!!!!!!

The fact of the matter though was that I was feeling so bad and with the situation I was in, I really had no choice. So I acquiesced and agreed to get the shot. He shot the needle in my arm and he left. My mind was racing with all kinds of fucked up thoughts, fears and imaginings going through my head. Before long I was sound asleep. I slept for 17 hours straight and missed the next days tour.

When I awoke 17 hours later, I felt like new money. Like a brand new Nigga! The flu and all of its symptoms were totally gone. I felt refreshed, renewed and energized. That doctor was a bad muthaphucka!!! He got a Nigga right!! From that point on I was able to truly enjoy every minute of my first trip to Africa.

Tuesday, June 26, 2018

Goals are being accomplished daily. When I look back to where I was when I got released from prison to where I am now … I have made tremendous progress. My mind tries to fuck wit me sometimes and tell me that I'm not where I "should be", but I offer a rebuttal to that muthaphucka and say "I'm right where I'm supposed to be". Things take time. My success is assured! Without a doubt at all. I'm too disciplined. I'm too focused. I'm too determined. I'm too patient. I'm too strong for it not to happen as I want it to.

Did my whole window cleaning route today, picked Lil Sean up from school. It was his last day. We are headed to the carnival at Giants Stadium.

I must keep going. I have to keep going. I will keep going.

Be True!   Be Bold!   Be Aggressive!

Sunday, July 1, 2018

We have to continually monitor ourselves. Our motives, expectations, thoughts, decisions, reactions, behaviors and execution. And when wrong or underperforming, we must make the necessary adjustments and changes to get us back on track and focused on where we are going. As I've said before, "The Mistake Family" is huge and there are a lot of them to contend with and we have to minimize our interactions with that family.

As long as we are alive and human we will always have confrontations with The Mistake Family, but we must try to always meet "new" members of that family. No sense in having altercations with the same old Mistake Family members over and over and over again.

Gotta stay determined and focus on my progress I've made so far and know that if I keep staying disciplined and focused, I will get to where I want to go….. in due time!

Peace out!

Be True!   Be Bold!   Be Aggressive

Monday, July 2, 2018

This shit don't stop!! You have to always be prepared, enthused, energetic and determined to make your world what you want it to be. The responsibility is mine and mine alone for my life and my existence in This Universe. I can't blame any person or any external circumstance for "my own condition". I am responsible for my life. My physical existence here on this planet is brief, short and finite. It will end. I will end. So for the time being, I have to build and construct my life how I want it to be.

Ain't no cry baby shit ova here!!

Be True!   Be Bold!   Be Aggressive

Wednesday, July 4, 2018

Progress is being made daily; by the hour; by the minute; by the second. I have to always remind myself of same so as to not slip into thoughts and feelings that things aren't happening fast enough. Everything in it's due time and right season. All of the "life experiences" that take place on the road to my goals are necessary ingredients to make the finished product sound and tight.

So much has been accomplished since my release from federal prison. Got my own apartment, wrote and self-published 2 books (working on the 3rd), started my own window cleaning business, filed for bankruptcy and got confirmed, started back trading options through my own account, started a YouTube Channel and so much more but the most important is that I AM 100% Full Time in Sean X. Gunby Jr's life (My Sun). That's the main thing.

I have decided to make a lot of money again. Up to this point I've just been chillin' enjoying my life and not too focused on making a whole bunch of money. I'm cool with my income and I keep my expenses to a minimum so as to not put a whole lot of pressure on me.

However, unlike 10 – 20 years ago, I now have a different perspective and view point on money, wealth and it's uses. Now, I see it as a means for me to have "choices" and "options" for my life and for Lil Sean and his kids. Whereas before, 10 -20 years ago I was on some "money equals success shit". I was so far away from the center. It took for me to lose it all to understand this. There would have been no way for a break-through to have been achieved in changing my psychology or philosophy about money, wealth and it's uses.

There are some things that I want to do before I am too old to do them. I am 49 years old and in tremendous physical shape so I am able to do it. I am discarding some things and people out of my life so that I can focus on amassing financial wealth. It's time. I'm ready. I can do it. I will do it! I will be a millionaire again.

Shut the fuck up and git to work!

Be True!   Be Bold!   Be Aggressive

Monday, July 9, 2018

This thing called "life" is very fragile and there are no guarantees from one day to the next. Each day must be lived to the fullest and dreams and goals moved on daily with aggression. I get caught up sometimes with "this and that"; shit that is really insignificant and a waste of time. I try not to stay there too too long and get de-focused. I catch myself and get right back to the mission at hand which is to SUCCEED and make my COMEBACK!

That's what this shit is all about. Overcoming adversity, surmounting difficulties, learning from failures and pushing forward toward the dream. It's not easy and it's not hard. It just is.

Be True!   Be Bold!   Be Aggressive

Tuesday, July 17, 2018

My life gets more and more interesting with each passing day. These books that I wrote and writing now are introducing me to all kinds of people from all walks of life. Somehow my book has gotten in the hands of an inmate on death row at San Quentin Prison in San Quentin, California. Amazing! Spoke to the brother on the phone and he said he liked the book.

I plan on keeping in contact with the Brutha 'cause I know how important and necessary it is for an inmate to have a pen pal and a connection to the outside world. For someone on death row, I would imagine that that is magnified 40x. So I plan to stay in touch with him.

I am in tremendous shape to do whatever I want. I am lucky. I am surrounded by opportunity and I have the freedom to move on these opportunities. No wasted movements. No wasted time. No wasted conversations. No wasted days. Every muthaphuckin' day must count for something.

Be grateful for what you have Sean and where you are!

Friday, July 20, 2018

It's 8:05am. I'm up and I'm at 'em! I will make this another successful day. I have my itinerary written down as to what I have to do today and will complete every task.

Focus is the key. Laser like focus on my goals. There are many I will achieve. There is no rush. I am patient and will knock them off 1-at-a-time. Some new and exciting things are happening that I've prepared for and I'm ready for them. I will be a millionaire again. Without a doubt!

My life is what I make it! And I'm going to make it a dynamic one.

Nothing is impossible for me!

Tuesday, July 24, 2018

It's 8:18am. I'm up and uploaded a video to my YouTube Channel, editing another video as I type, had my coffee, boiled corn on the cob, checking my options positions and seeing what the market is doing. Once I'm done with this, I'll be out the door to knock out my window cleaning route for today.

I'm working on somethin' in my life and it feels good. I'm going somewhere and it feels good. I have a destination and it feels good. I have a plan and it feels good. I'm in motion and it feels good. I have discipline and it feels good. I'm in good physical fitness shape and it feels good. I'm excellent mentally and it feels good. I'm at peace spiritually and it feels good.

I make my world what I want it to be! I have a right to My Life!

Peace out!

Thursday, July 26, 2018

Hit a snag in a personal relationship of mines and it got real intense emotionally. However, this being said and this being the case, I won't let myself get bogged down with sorrow, lament, grief, remorse or trying to "fix" the situation. I must still keep pushing forward in spite of. I must still stay on my course. I must still follow my map. I must still follow my plan. I must still stay focused. I must still stay disciplined. This doesn't stop. I will continue to move forward.

I caused someone some harm and pain. Not intentional, but nonetheless, I did. I apologized. My apology was sincere and I will make amends if I am able to.

Went out this morning and did my Thursday route and now I'm back home relaxing and chilling a minute until I go back out this afternoon to finish the 2nd phase of my route.

Adversity, setbacks and negative situations don't paralyze me anymore like they used to. I am so focused and have prepared myself so thoroughly that I "shake that shit off" quick and keep my head to the sky. I can remember when these situations would devastate, immobilize and crush me to the point where I wouldn't want to do anything except lay down and lament about how fucked up my life was and highlight everything that was wrong with my life. I don't do this any longer. I'm stronger now. I'm tougher now. I'm truer now. I'm a man now...(in the truest sense of the word).

It feels good.

I will continue onward toward my destination without a doubt.

Saturday, July 28, 2018

I'm doing "my own thang"!!. Fuck what the world or anyone else wants me to do. I'm doing my own thing. I am one individual. I am one human being. I am unique. I am different. There is no other human being on the planet similar or an exact replica of me. Henceforth, and for ever more, I will "be me". I will celebrate my uniqueness. I will self-celebrate my existence. I will cheer myself on at all times. When I find myself going against myself I will take immediate corrective action to repair whatever defect there is inside of me.

Today was another Awesome day! That seems to be all that I have is "Awesome days". Finished my entire window cleaning route for the day. Worked out (10 sets of 10's on pull ups, push ups and dips). Cleaned my Lil Sean's and my fish tank with fresh new water. Filmed some more videos for my YouTube Channel. And now I'm writing on my book. Today was a Success!

Peace out!

Sunday, July 29, 2018

Everything is love! Did a 10 mile bike ride this morning first thing and got that shit out the way. A Nigga feelin' good and energetic and ready to tackle the world. Picking my little man up from the airport today this afternoon I guess. I think he missed his flight coming back so I'm waiting to see what the deal is.

Anyway, life is moving forward and my dreams and goals are materializing and manifesting right before my eyes. Adversity is still common and forever present and that is ok. Adversity makes me sharper and more determined and focused. One day at a time. One inch at a time. Patience is the money. The ability to wait is the money.

Peace out!

Monday, July 30, 2018

Don't feel right today! Don't fuckin' feel right. That's because something is not right with my thoughts. The thought creates the emotion.

I had a female disrespect me, my son, my house and another friend of mine and I couldn't do nothing about it. I had to eat it. I'm still eating it and it doesn't taste good. She spit in my face. She spit in my face. I couldn't do a thing. I have to ALWAYS consider the ramifications and effects of my decisions, choices and ultimate actions. I understand fully that I am a Black American Male in the United States. I am a convicted felon. The male always loses in domestic violence situations. The mental energy needed to extract myself from a situation like that would take away from my other responsibilities that are way more important.

I understand all this.

Shit still don't feel good.

I want to whoop somebody's ass and show a Nigga don't fuck wit me like that. Don't fuckin' fuck wit me like that bitch!

I can't.

I won't.

I will think better tomorrow.

I will feel better tomorrow.

Tuesday, July 31, 2018

A better day today. What a difference a day makes. 86,400 seconds ago I was not thinking and consequently feeling as good as I'm feeling now. You gotta keep moving and see what the end is going to be. You have to keep going no matter what. It doesn't stop. Striving for my goals requires constant dedication and focus. Determination is tantamount to the accomplishment of any goal. You have to want it. I has to be a burning desire. IT HAS TO BE A BURNING DESIRE!!. You can't fuck around with it. Fuckin' piddle-paddle around with shit. You have to fuckin' MOVE ON IT! TODAY! RIGHT NOW! Not tomorrow. NOW!!

Get to work!

Peace out

Wednesday, August 01, 2018

Keep pushing forward no matter what! Every day is not going to be sunshine. Some days will be dark. We need those dark days to sharpen us, ready us and remind us that the work is never complete. It's survival of the fittest in this world. You are on your own. Nobody is coming to help you. You must help yourself! I will help me. I am there for me. I will aide and comfort me. I got me. I got it!

Tuesday, August 07, 2018

I'm up and things are looking up in my life. I have some deals working that will provide me with the capital to elevate my financial life above where it is now. I've made a decision to cut back on and eliminate some activities in my life that had become a distraction for what I'm doing. I had "too many minds". Too many different things going on at the same time and this is never good. For me to get to where I want to go, it requires a tremendous amount of discipline, focus and hard work. I would love to "skate" in the easy way and get what I want that way….but that shit is fantasy. One has to be pushing all the time. Dedicated, determined, focused, disciplined, strong, rested, sharp, in excellent physical condition, no bad energy hampering the spirit and you must have a plan.

Money!

Sunday, September 02, 2018

Excellence. Excellence. That's the word for the moment. Excellence. I exhibit this. I practice this. I think this therefore I feel this. I speak this therefore I become this. I live this. I envision this. I create this. I embody this. I am this. I will be this. I will always be this. I expect this. I give this. I perform this. I speak this. I demand this. I can see this. I can spot this. I demonstrate this.

I am Excellence.

Thursday, September 06, 2018

Just Keep Goin'!!

Don't look back to beat yourself up for the mistakes you have made and where you are not that you think you should be. Don't look back to admire your work, success and progress that you have made from all the work that you've put in.

Just keep goin'! Keep movin' forward! Don't stop for no one! Don't wait for no one! Just keep goin'! You will get the chance one day to sit back and admire your work….just not today or tomorrow. The day will come. You will enjoy the fruit juices of your labor. You will sit under the shade of the work you have put in. You will pick from your garden from all the seeds that you have planted…..just not today or tomorrow.

Just keep goin'!

Thursday, September 13, 2018

Slow Down And Calm Down!!

I have allowed myself to become disheartened and frustrated with my process and my plan. It is not happening fast enough and I'm being reckless trying to rush my comeback. I just need to slow the fuck down and take a deep breath and remember who the fuck I am and how far I have come. This is not a sprint. It's a marathon. And the one who could last the longest and has the biggest gas tank will win. That will be me.

Woke up this morning and was not feeling my current circumstances. But then as the day went on and I started to look forward (instead of looking backwards); my day got progressively better and I created a renewed energy and raised my own vibration by myself. I be doin' that shit. I'll raise my own muthaphuckin' vibration when I get ready. I don't need nobody's permission to raise my own shit. This my shit. I control and master my vibration.

My best days are in front of me.

Be True!   Be Bold!   Be Aggressive!

Saturday, September 29, 2018

It Don't Stop!!

I'm up and at 'em! Another good day is here. It will be another positive and productive day for sure. Got some videos to shoot lined up down in Lincoln Park in Jersey City then I may go clean some windows later.

I am doing a much better job with my trading since I've stopped "over trading" and trying to "rush my plan". When I take my time I have better results. I am slowly building my capital base that I will need to really take flight and execute some other plans that I have. I owe a few people some money that I intend on repaying so that I can get those thoughts off my spirit and out of my mind. This will be less "mental clutter" and will allow my spiritual and mental engine to run even smoother.

I'm still eating clean and exercising 5 – 6 days a week which makes all the difference in my mental attitude. I dread working out some days but "I just go" to the track and "start" and once I've started then I'm money and glad I went.

I got a good life!

Just Because It's Not Moving Fast Doesn't Mean I'm Not Progressing!!

Most times I have to "slow my own mind down" and tell myself to relax and chill. That just because I'm not at my final destination or close to achieving my ultimate goal ..this doesn't mean that I'm not moving forward and on my way there. Just because I experience a little adversity or suffer a minor reverse or setback doesn't mean that I'm not on my way.

As long as I'm "up and doing", "moving and shaking" and pushing forward, then everything is alright. It's supposed to be uncomfortable. It's supposed to be frustrating. The journey is supposed to be tiresome. There is supposed to be some doubt. All these are necessary evils to forever remind me of where I've come and what I went through to achieve my ultimate goals and build my life the way I want it to be.

I must also "remember to remember" where I've came from and all the progress I have made to date. I have come a long way since getting released from prison. I've made some HUGE strides and am well on my way to where I want to go. One of the primary benefits that I focus on is that at 49 years old, I am still young, mentally acute, physically solid and spiritually centered. As long as I've got these the money will come in due time.

Yes, I'm back after the money now. Not for the sake of accumulating as much as I can to brag and boast or show off, but instead to be able to do the things I want to do with my family. Additionally, to be able to spread the message that you can make a comeback from any situation if you believe in yourself. That you can bounce back better and stronger than you were before. That you need failure and adversity in order to give birth to a newer, fresher, stronger and more robust self.

The Phoenix flies!

Off My Game!

I got off my game waiting, expecting and depending on someone else to do something for me that they said they were going to do for me. Namely, invest in me financially to the tune of $25,000. This would've allowed me to fall back big time from my window cleaning business and focus more on selling my books and trading options. Needless to say it never came through and when I looked up I saw myself way off my discipline game. Off my focus game. Off my concentration game. Off my creativity game.

It's OK. Another lesson learned. Never git off yo game Sean!! Don't let up on your set up Sean! Don't allow yourself to be distracted Sean! I got off my own plan depending on another muthaphucka! Bad poker Sean! You know better! Go out and earn your own $25,000. Move and create your own good fortune to bring yourself $25,000. Depend on Sean to give Sean $25,000. You can do it! Make that Shit happen!

Thursday, October 11, 2018

I'm starting all over again. Got myself into a financial tight spot due to my lack of discipline and proper planning. It's my fault. I did this. It was necessary though because now it forces me to "tighten up" and "git right" in all areas of my life. No more will I allow what someone promises me or says what they will do for me to get me to "lighten up" on my game plan. I forgot to "don't let up on my set up". Always keep my plan and my course of action #1 in my life. Stay on track. Stay focused.

I have to do better and I can. I have it in me to do better and I will.

Saturday, October 13, 2018

What am I afraid of? Because I've taken some losses in the market now I'm scared. That's a Part of the game Sean. If big hedge funds consistently take losses then you will take some losses. Everybody takes losses in the market. The goal is to limit your losses and not let them run. So what am I afraid of? I went to school for just this career. I trained for it. I prepared for it day and night. I slept it. I breathed it. I ate it. I dreamt it. I fucked it. I kissed it. I am ready.

I know that one of the obstacles is that I have "too many minds" going on at the same time. I have to limit the number of minds I have. I can't be doing YouTube videos, cleaning windows, editing videos, shooting videos, traveling to video shoots, being a Professional Black Father and trading at the same time. Trading has to be my Primary Focus! Trading is not a hobby. Trading is a tough tough business and requires 100% dedication and concentration. Trading is going to bring me the lifestyle that I want to live. Trading is going to help me do the things I want to do for Lil Sean and my posterity. Trading can bring me this. I can do it. I'm ready and I'm prepared. I've done the work and I am willing to keep working. Now is the time to put my all into it.

Monday, October 15, 2018

Here we go! This shit don't stop! Fuck it….start all over … Plan it out.. think it through and then GET TO WORK! Be patient. Don't rush it Sean. Take your time and hit your target. Fuck trying to help the world. The 1st law of nature is "self-preservation". Take care of you and Lil Sean.

Get your shit together and then do the things that you want to do. Bring that shit into fruition. Manifest that shit. Manifest your thoughts into "real world reality". Concentrate, focus, discipline and control your thoughts to only what is material and relevant toward your effecting your destiny. Fuck everything and everyone else. No time for bullshit acquaintances. No time for bullshit meaningless conversations. No time for wasted energy, movements or time. Everything has to count for something. Every move is a kill move!

You got it Nigga.. Believe it and make it happen!

Peace out!

Friday, November 02, 2018

When you have already shown yourself that you can achieve (i.e. past successes, past goal accomplishments) then it's much easier to believe and know that you can do it again. This is a personal thing, an internal thing. My tendency in my life has been to try and prove to someone and everyone else that I can achieve and to seek their approval and applause for my progress. This is a bad philosophy as when you are seeking the approval of someone or everyone else and you allow yourself to get to the point to where someone else's and everyone else's approval becomes the primary focal point and tantamount in how "you judge your own progress an success" then I am fucked.

Because you will never get everyone's approval 100% of the time. You will always get someone or maybe even everyone's disapproval. Then what? This is bad philosophy and a terrible mindset to have because everyone's values system is different even amongst those in the same group. All people have different intellectual aptitudes, different expectations, different viewpoints, different outlooks, different mental attitudes and has had different "life experiences", which in turn shape their opinions, values and belief systems. So why then do I allow myself so much as 3 minutes of concerning myself with the approval of anyone other than MYSELF!?

I know me better than anyone. I know my capabilities better than anyone. I lived through all of my "life experiences" with me, I was there for the whole movie. I know my goals, aspirations and dreams. I alone am the judge of my progress. I alone am the "worker of the scale" to determine my rightness or wrongness. I alone will sit on the scale to be weighed by The Universe. Hence, my opinion of me and my actions and my approval of me is of most importance.

The Black American Male Is A Broken Man

Broken – 1. Split or cracked into pieces; splintered, fractured, burst, etc. 2. Not in working condition; out of order. 3. Not kept or observed; violated. 4. Sick, weakened or beaten. 5. Bankrupt 6. Not complete. 7. Subdued and trained; tamed

This man is broken. He is broken in every facet and every expression of the word "broken" and fits the aforementioned definition exactly. I must clarify that when I speak of the Black American Male being broken, I do not mean "individually" on an individual basis. However, conversely, I mean the Black American Male "collectively" or a as a collective group.

This man has been damaged, scarred and wounded to the depths of his soul, so much so, that he has abandoned himself and his right to his own life. His self-abandonment has fostered a level of self-hatred and self-rejection so deep that it is extremely difficult to diagnose and consequently almost impossible to come up with a prognosis to remedy his illness. His spiritual damage is total and complete to the point where he has ran away from his own soul and the very essence of who he is as a unique human being. His mental wounds have been extremely severe for centuries and are so deep seated that it has driven him into denial of current condition.

This man is lost and what's most tragic is that he seems incapable of finding himself on his own. He won't help himself. He won't even try to make a concerted effort to improve himself and his quality of life. He seems to have no concept of the Universal fact that "he has a right to his life" in this Universe given to him not by another man but by The Sun, The Moon and The Stars. It is often times embarrassing to be a Black American Male. It is often times shameful to be a Black American Male.

I am a Black American Male and I am proud to be one and I wouldn't have it any other way and wouldn't want to be anyone else.

Monday, November 03, 2018

The Mindset of a Champion

Man..he is not concerned with nothing but achieving, winning and overcoming. He will not be deterred, discouraged or impeded from his priority, which is to be a Champion. He is not concerned with his current circumstances, he is not lamenting about his past or current life, he is focused on "where he will be" in the future. He is currently and actively creating his future.

He has fixed his brokenness. He eradicates all weakness as soon as they appear, immediately. He eliminates all distractions and monitors his behavior and his performance in his own life. He is super critical of Himself, not to beat himself down, but to sharpen hisself and elevate his game. He doesn't get involved or mixed up in bullshit or deal with weak ass people. He is comfortable in "his own" skin and doesn't need acceptance from anyone other than himself. He stands alone secure in himself. He gets right to the heart of every matter, he doesn't fuck around with colorful conversations with loquacious people who talk around issues rather getting straight to the utmost important point. He has no time to waste. He is extremely careful about his time, vibration and energy.

He don't fuck around. He is a Champion.

Monday, November 05, 2018

I'm up and at 'em! Another day will be won. I will be victorious again today. Nobody on the planet today will out think me, out discipline me, out focus me, out concentrate me, out work me. I command my vibration and my thoughts. Therefore I am master of my world, my Universe and ultimately my life, destiny and legacy.

Only A Fool Prepares Himself On The Battlefield

A Brutha named "Cunningham" told me this when I was in the joint. It seems and sounds so elementary, however, I was 46 years old and had never even thought about it or pondered it. It was profound to me at that moment. It was apropos for where I was in my life at that time. It made so much sense. Considering my current condition at that time, having lost everything that I owned material and otherwise, being in federal prison and planning my comeback, this was penicillin to my broken and fractured mental state.

It would take planning to make my comeback. I needed to think through my forward-life. Where was I? Where did I want to go? Where was I going? How was I going to get there? What was the best most efficient route to arriving at where I wanted to ultimately end up? How do I do it?

"Only A Fool Prepares Himself On The Battlefield"

I immediately saw the absolute truth in this statement and at once began to pontificate, visualize, ponder, think and write my "battle plan", i.e, strategy. It felt good. I instantly became empowered with a confidence I never before had. I instantly became emboldened and imbued with the belief and knowledge that whatever the fuck I wanted to do…. I could and would do it. I felt a new found level of self-control that made me know that "my life was my own" and that "I had a right to my life" and that it was completely in my own mind as to what I could and would do with it. I began to like myself again. My fractured mind began to develop scabs and began the healing process. My broken spirit was immediately put into a cast and began to repair itself. I was on my way back.

No longer would I live my life recklessly, carelessly in a haphazard manner allowing myself to be blown about by the winds of whim, misdirection and "uncalculated" chance taking. My life and my thoughts would now forever be thought out and planned and I would "take my time" and be patient with myself.

If I planned beforehand I had a 6,000% chance of better results than if I didn't plan, even if the plan didn't work and failed. If it didn't work, I would just go back to my original plan and see what and where I went wrong.

You have to plan Sean. You have to have a plan to do what you are going to do. If you plan Sean, you are assured of arriving at your pre-planned destination and can't no muthaphucka stop it!

Thursday, November 08, 2018

I Survived It!

As I think happens with all people who have been fucked over, betrayed or crossed by someone close to them but not "really" being 1,000% sure of the details and as the days go by and events happen, situations occur, peoples behavior towards you and things begin to reveal themselves…the picture becomes clearer and clearer and those old feelings comeback of anger, shock and disbelief.

It takes you back years to the moment when the whole shit went down and you re-live that shit and re-play that shit back in your mind again and again and again and again until you realize "oohhh shit"...that muthaphucka! Then revenge sets in and blinds you telling you that it is the only course of action. That revenge must be exacted upon the guilty party or parties. This may be true and is a valid response. I leave that up to you.

But I have to play the tape all the way through and look at the weak muthaphuckas who did what they did to me. Look at their lives, events that have happened in their lives and how weak and broken they are and how fucked up their lives are at the moment (even years later), and see that "they didn't get over", maybe on me, but not The Sun, Moon and Stars. You can never get one by The Universe. It sees everything.

When I sit back and contemplate how far I've come in such a short period and see all of my successes I "dig" myself and analyze my life now and my future and I know that I will comeback stronger than ever and that will be my revenge. I won't fuck up and put myself in a situation where I will ever be separated from My Sun again.

When I look at it from that perspective I won!

I survived it! I survived it!

That's what matters most. I'm still muthaphuckin' here!

I survived it!

Wednesday, November 14, 2018

Something is not right

I'm off. My thinking. The way I'm viewing myself. My mood. My enthusiasm is gone. My motivation is low. I've taken some big losses in the options markets and I'm down on myself. I'm disappointed in my performance thus far. I can do better. I'm not performing up to my potential. I'm not exercising patience nor discipline in my trading. Trading takes laser focus, discipline and patience all working in tandem with knowledge and self-confidence.

At this point i'm not motivated to clean windows and would rather trade full time, however, I'm not properly capitalized with Enough capital. This being so and me not exercising patience, I'm taking too much risk hoping for the BIG trade to get me properly capitalized. The result is that these low probability trades that I'm putting on routinely fail at a greater rate than they succeed, hence, I lose all of my money.

I know empirically that high probability trades is the proper course of action and provide the best chance for success. However, with my small stack, it will undoubtedly take a long time to build my stack to where I will eventually be properly capitalized, and I haven't been able to exercise the requisite patience and discipline to effect this strategy. It is the winning strategy. This I know for a fact as I've already lost over $500,000 following the high-risk low probability strategy 5 – 6 years ago. I know that Shit don't work so why do I still expect it to now.

I'm rushing. I want to be rich again right away. I want to be rich immediately. I don't want to wait anymore. In a strange way I even feel as though I'm entitled to be rich again without putting in the requisite work. Word up! I feel that way. I want to be rich while I'm still young, look good and still have A lot of energy so I'm rushing. And failing right along.

What's the solution?

Calm down, slow down, take my time. There is no hurry. Write down and study my strategy and maxim's that I wrote down while I was at FCI Morgantown go back and really study those, breathe those, live those and implement them muthaphucka's in my trading going forward. If I do that alone, my success rate and longevity will increase instantly 3-fold.

It's possible.

Martin Luther King, Jr.'s Advocacy For Black America's Integration Into Mainstream White America Is Wholly Responsible For Black America's Abandonment Of Itself

I was born in America in 1969 and matriculated through my early childhood life in the 1970's and 1980's in America and I distinctly remember visibly seeing Black Americans having "soul" and our own "Black Culture" within but without white America. It was pervasive throughout North Jersey where I grew up and down south as well when I would visit on occasion.

"Sean, what do you mean "soul" and "Black culture"?"

What I speak of is a vibe, a feel, a look, an expression of pride, a uniqueness, an energy that permeated everyday Black life in America. Back during the 1970's Black people had "soul" and were proud that they had soul and seemed to do everything imaginable and possible to express and protect that "soul". Black Americans, the overwhelming majority, in no way shape or form wanted to be associated with any other culture, they acknowledged, loved and embraced their terminal uniqueness, their "Blackness", defended it with ferocity, expressed it with a superfluous amount of confidence and pride and didn't want to be anything other than themselves.

This was evident and could be seen with the way they walked, talked, dressed, their styles of fashion, the erectness of their backbone, the uprightness of their shoulders, their heads to the sky and the internal "fight and will to live" that showed through their countenance and body language. Black America embraced their culture, customs, ideas and past-history, which largely took place in the southern region of America. Many of those Black southern customs, traditions, thought processes, ideas, mannerisms, learned behaviors were brought to the northern cities during the great migration of southern Black Americans moving north for better economic opportunities and to escape the prisoner of war oppression in the south.

Even though Black Americans didn't measure up from an economic standpoint with white America, it was ok because we "had our own thang" about us which made us proud and most importantly we had a self-love of our own culture. This is better than money in my opinion. With this fostering of our "own thang" we had more Black banks, insurance companies, doctors, dentists, professionals, restaurants and businesses since it was pretty much mandated that we transact business with each other. From this Black economics would flourish and thrive and be self-sustaining.

Even the images that we saw on TV in the 1970's of Black Americans were spiritually and mentally empowering and stimulating. When you watched Soul Train, Sanford and Son, The Jeffersons, Good Times, What's Happening, Fat Albert & The Cosby Kids, Jackson 5 cartoon, etc., you saw the unadulterated, unfiltered and true expression of Black America emanating from the television screen. And when you saw this, what was supremely apparent and clear was that Black America was cool and had "soul".

Even when you watched a TV show that had a largely white cast and would have a token Brutha or Sista on the show to capture a larger audience, even that lone Brutha or Sista would radiate their Black American "soul" on the screen. Examples would be The Mod Squad, Barney Miller, Different Strokes, Give Me A Break, Starsky & Hutch, etc.

On Saturday mornings, to watch an episode of "The Soul Train", was to be taken on a expedition into the truest expression and essence of what it was to be a Black American. The looks on the faces, the dance, the Afros, the clothes, the style, the swagger, Don Corneilus' way of speak, dress, moves and style all said "Say It Loud, I'm Black And I'm Proud". To watch Fred G. Sanford be a man amongst men and advocate for his self-respect as a Black man was a classroom in itself. The father James on Good Times was Black American Male masculinity at the highest level and it was always shown that he was the spinal cord of that household in the Cabrini Green Housing Projects in Chicago, IL. George Jefferson's boldness and self-confidence about his blackness was evident in every episode. All of these shows embodied the mental security that we were proud to be who we were and didn't want to be white or assimilate into any other culture but our own.

There is not stronger point to be made about this topic than the Black American music, musicians and artists of the 1970's – 1980's who personified what it was to have "soul". The inflection of the voices, the vernacular, the black drawl of the English language, the clothes, the dance, the self-expression, the Afros, the style...THE SOUL. This was all borne out the Black American experience of isolation and self-containment here in America and never has there been any music or artistry that captures that more succinctly than the music of the 1960's, 1970's and 1980's. I don't think there ever will be again.

This music had "soul" and was "feeling" music. Motown, Aretha Franklin, Curtis Mayfield, Wilson Pickett, James Brown, The O'Jays, Jackson 5, Michael Jackson, Roberta Flack, Gladys Knight & The Pips, David Ruffin, Stevie Wonder, the list goes on and on and on, Johnny Taylor, Otis Redding, Bill Withers, Sly & The Family Stone, all of this music had "soul" as it was called "Soul Music".

All of the aforementioned artists, actors, muscians, etc were either born before or raised by someone who lived before the push for integration by Martin Luther King, Jr., hence, their expression of their "soul" drew upon that experience of pre-integration self-containment.

Then Dr. King came along espoused the theory of Black America's integration into a white America that cringed at the prospect of sharing with its prisoner of war, that rebelled against the idea of ever being equal to it's captives and fought tirelessly against the notion of ever assimilating and comingling with Black America. Yet Dr. King thought it a good strategy and espoused all of the benefits that would accrue to Black America as a whole and this utopian fantasy for all of the citizens of America both Black and white. Not to go on a long diatribe about all of the implications and results of this failed experiment (which I touched upon briefly in aSTIGMAtism In My Soul – Volume I), but keeping on topic as to this being the main reason that caused Black America to abandon itself.

Today it's November 18, 2018, just look at Black America take a really good look and tell me what you see.

Yes I understand "evolving" and that civilizations go through evolutions resulting in changes to those cultures and civilizations, but those cultures, even though they progress technologically, economically, artistically, etc., make sure their core culture or "soul" is protected and kept wholly intact.

My position remains that Dr. King's thesis of integration has proven itself to be a complete and utter catastrophe and failure. That Dr. King's trumpeting of integration asphyxiated Black American culture, Black American uniqueness, Black American "soul" and propelled us to abandon ourselves and "our own thang".

Hence, we are where we are.

Peace out!

The United States of America's Prison Industrial Complex And It's Impact On The Black American Male And His Family

In these United States of America, there is what's known as "The Prison Industrial Complex", which, was set up to "warehouse" human beings for extended periods of time. There are many reasons as to why The Prison Industrial Complex was invented and I will not attempt to ascertain and front like I really do know why. Being a Black American Male of 49 years, I would hypothesize and say that one of the foundational and underlying reasons is economical. Some kind of way there is an economic benefit to the USA or else this project would have never taken flight. Isn't this, the United States of America, a capitalistic society? "In name" at least.

Today, we will examine the negative impact The Prison Industrial Complex has on its own citizenry, more specifically, The Black American Male.

The overwhelming majority of the inmates or prisoners "warehoused" in America's city jails, county jails, state prisons and penitentiaries and federal prisons and penitentiaries are Black American Males. There has been much empirical and practical research done with statistical exactness to support these findings. I myself know this from a real and practical level as I've been inside city jails, county jails and federal prison. So I speak from real world experience. In every case when I've been inside, Black American Males outnumbered and represented the largest percentage of every other ethnic group present in the jail or prison.

The Soul Destruction Of The Black American Male

From ages 15 – 40, The Black American Male is well represented in The Prison Industrial Complex. Yes, 41 years old and up as well but I want to stay in the lower age ranges to drive home my points of interest. This age range of, 15 – 40, is any male ethnic group of any race, creed, color, etc., "prime child creation" years when the young male is in the prime of his life, his most productive years from an economic/work standpoint, his mental acuity and lucidness is sharpest, his physical fitness abilities and capabilities are at their apex and these years signify his most aggressive posture and behavior.

When the Black American Male is removed (or removes himself?) from his-self, his family and his community and becomes a guest in The Prison Industrial Complex, there is a hole blown through himself, his family and his community that thwarts overall stability, growth and maintenance of the Black American family. Essentially, that becomes the end of the Black American Male (for the time he is incarcerated), his family and his community. The spinal cord, the heart, the cerebral cortex and mouth of the Black American family has been asphyxiated and put to death.

The Black American Male, while a guest in The Prison Industrial Complex, does not contribute anything economically or financially to his family but instead becomes a burden to his family, a now 1 parent household, as they now have to raise money to send to him inside for his sustenance and survival inside. He needs to buy food from commissary, make phone calls and other things which require more money than his "prison job" can pay for. So what little resources the mother of his children earns has to be shared with him without his contributing anything to the family. This is economic and financial annihilation to his family. This germinates, fosters and enflames poverty in the mother of his children, the children and household leading to stress, lack, low self-esteem and other psychological ailments that come with poverty and his being absent from the equation. This has a tremendously negative impact on The Black American Male and his family.

The Soul Destruction Of The Black American Male's Son

The Black American Male, while a guest in The Prison Industrial Complex, effectively destroys his children, especially the Black American Boy child, his son. The Black American daughter suffers too as a result of his absence but not as acutely and intensely as the Black American Boy child.

Without the physical presence, wisdom, guidance and discipline of the Black American father, the little boy is doomed and in a fucked-up situation. The little Black American Male boy needs to hear that "bass in the voice" of the Black American Male father to know that he has a leader in his life. A leader that "knows him", "knows what he is about to encounter as a Black American Male" in America, "is him" and "loves him".

The Black American father is not there to provide love and support, teach courage, create and augment self-love, self-respect, self-discipline and self-esteem. As a guest in The Prison Industrial Complex, his is incapable of learning his son the crucial points of overcoming failures, the finer details of surmounting adversity and that he should confront his fears versus shrinking from them. He cannot impart wisdom on how to be responsible, self-sufficient, independent, to know right from wrong and how to be a leader.

He is not there to "make him get up" and not "pick him up" when he gets knocked down whether self-inflicted or done by an external force. He is not there to lecture him on "fake friendships", "true friendships", "family", relationships with girls, dealing with white people, dealing with good white people, dealing with crackas, being a Black Man in a white mans world, how to walk, how to talk, making eye contact when speaking to another person especially another man, the importance of evaluating body language, The Universe, God and ultimately any topic of interest that may arise in his lifetime.

The little boy is left to fend for himself and learn what little he can from the females in his life whether they be his mother, sisters, grand-mothers, aunts, etc. These female family members no matter how earnest and true they may be at attempting to "raise a little Black American boy to be a man", they are grossly insufficient and without being intentional, indirectly accentuate his becoming weak and effeminate, especially mentally. This leads to the little Black American boys becoming quitters and easily influenced by outside mediums in their search for wholeness and purpose. Effectively, what happens here is that this little Black American boy, through no fault of his own, will as a result of his father being missing, increase his probability of becoming a guest in The Prison Industrial Complex thereby repeating the cycle for generations to come.

The Soul Destruction Of The Black American Male's Daughter

The Black American Male, while a guest in The Prison Industrial Complex, effectively destroys his children, especially the Black American Boy child, his son. The Black American daughter suffers tremendously without the Black American father as she talks, behaves and

The Alpha Male Lion That Has No Teeth And No Fight

Can you imagine what life must be like for the most robust, stout and physically imposing lion in Kruger National Park, the Serengeti, Sabi Sands or the Massai Mara, that has no teeth and no fight. This lion wanders around the plains and landscape of a vast area being less than himself. His shoulders are slumped, his head is down and his eyes display a weakness that penetrates to his soul. The other lions ridicule him and view him with massive feelings of condescension and hold him in utter contempt. They make a mockery of him. He is the butt of all the jokes and garners no respect from the other lions.

All the other animals (wildebeest, gazelles, oryx, buffalo, warthog) of which he holds dominion are well aware of who he is, they shrink in his presence and are acutely on guard for their lives because they know his position in the ecosystem. Yet, over time, for hundreds of years, after having witnessed his body language, his actions, his behavior and his self-imposed low self-perception of himself, they too discuss his weakness and secretly joke about what he has become. They haven't seen him make a kill ever and don't even run when he comes along. They no he has no teeth and no courage.

He has no pride (family), no lioness even considers him because he is mentally incapable of protecting her and being the patriarch of any type of pride. She would much rather be protected than having to be the protector. She knows her role as the lioness and does not wish to be the lion because she knows she can never be. She has seen the other lions abuse, misuse and beat him up repeatedly, hence, she too holds him in utter contempt. None of the lionesses have any type of respect for him. To them, he is a lost cause incapable of building, maintaining and sustaining any type dynasty.

This lion laments, wails and continues to destroy everything inside of himself by constantly brooding on the worst experiences of his life and how he lost his teeth, his will, his self-esteem, his self-confidence and his love of self. He remains bound by his past incapable of moving forward and achieving his rightful greatness in his domain. He won't fight. He won't turn the page. He won't get up off the mat and try again. He has grown accustomed to being treated as the outcast lion that he has now believes he is such. The ridicule, scorn, failures, setbacks and mistakes he has heard and suffered over the years has been indelibly engraved into his conscience and soul that he now thinks and feels that this is how things are supposed to be.

He begs for help from every other lion and animal as to how to fix himself. Most shun him and his presence. The animals that make themselves available to hear his cry for help, do so with ulterior motives and plans to take advantage of him and push his psyche further into oblivion. The very fact that an animal would make themselves available to him thrusts the lion into feelings of false-hope, temporary happiness and imagined acceptance. From this he begins to raise his opinion of himself. However, when the trickery, manipulation and deception are put into full effect by the other animals and the lion realizes what has happened AGAIN, mentally and spiritually he descends to lower lows, deeper hopelessness, destitution and despair. He eventually abandons himself.

This continues and continues and continues and continues and continues and continues and continues until one split second.

The lion gets tired of feeling the way he feels. The lion gets tired of thinking the way he thinks. The lion gets tired of abandoning himself. The lion gets tired of his appearance. The lion gets tired of his outlook on life. The lion gets tired of asking for help. The lion gets tired of waiting for someone or some thing outside of himself to help him.

The lion begins to look inward. The lion begins to examine himself deeply. The lion takes himself to task. The lion begins to blame himself for his condition. The lion begins to review and painfully examine his past behavior and mistakes. The lion begins to look at himself differently. The lion begins to think of himself differently which leads to him feeling differently about himself. The lion begins to look at himself versus the other lions and animals and sees very vividly his advantages and dominance over all and begins to believe again. The lion is growing in vision. The lion is dreaming BIG now. The lion is elevating his self-perception by himself. The lion raises his own self-esteem by himself. The lion is now self-confident beyond belief. His body language tells a different story. His eyes tell a different story. His shoulders are no longer slumped. His head is no longer down but upright and erect. His chest is poked out. He walk is one of supreme confidence. He has decided on his own to help himself. He has decided to take his place in his own life.

The lion is back.

The lion has sharp teeth and fangs and the bravery, will, fortitude, strength, spirit and determination. He is ready for war.

The Black American Male is the lion that has no teeth and no fight in 2019.

Friday, December 7, 2018

It's first thing in the morning, I've had my 2 cups of coffee, 3 boiled eggs and now I'm ready to advance. I'm back on my "going to sleep early – waking up early" routine and I see the difference in my performance and the way I feel. Had a good week this week. Got a lot of things accomplished.

Continuing to work on my vision. I'm taking my time. No need to rush. As long as I continue to get up and do the right things for the right reasons it will just be a matter of time before I arrive at my desired destination.

My attitude is great and I'm physically in tremendous shape.

All I do is keep moving forward … onward and upward!

Friday, December 14, 2018

Just had a dope cup of coffee and working on my 2nd cup! Shit taste good as a muthaphucka. I'm a coffee drinker. Love that shit. Right now I drink no less than 3 cups a day sometimes up to 5 or 6. Had me some fried ham and boiled eggs for my morning protein. Definitely going to work out today to keep this muthaphuckin' mind and body TIGHT!

You have to be energetic and aggressive in this life. You have to be forward-moving, focused and determined to create the kind of life you want for yourself while you can and are able. Especially in America, this place affords the greatest opportunity to be whomever you desire to be. So I take advantage of same.

I remain directed toward that vision in my mind of where I want to go. At 49 years old there is no time to be fucking around and half steppin'. Every move is a kill move! Every move must count. Every conversation must count. Every personal interaction with other human beings must count. Every thought that is thought must count as they will express themselves through act.

I make sure 1,000% that I remain in excellent physical condition so that I can last for the long haul. I eat clean foods primarily, I get 6 – 8 hours of sleep every night NO EXCEPTIONS! I have a plan written down of where I am going in my life. Every day I write out my "daily itinerary" of what the fuck I have to do on that particular day, this keeps me focused. With consistent almost daily exercise my mind stays SUPER SHARP and my body the same. The endorphins and dopamines in my brain get released creating real euphoria in my life expanding my vision of my capabilities and what I'm able to accomplish. This is supremely important.

Sleep and rest are the "regenerative mechanisms" NEEDED in order for me to operate at peak performance. Fuck that shit that you have to forgo sleep in order to be successful. BAD INFORMATION!!! Sleep deprivation is a torture technique used by military personnel when the capture an opposing enemy and want to get information/intelligence from him. They deprive him of sleep to the point to where he breaks and tells all just to rest his mind and body. The cognitive functions of our brains begin to diminish from lack of rest and sleep. The body needs rest as does the mind.

I'm ready as a muthaphucka!!

I stay ready so I don't have to get ready!

I got it!

Wednesday, December 26, 2018

Keep the pressure on! Keep the pressure up to maximum levels. The pressure must be kept on me by me. I have to push me. I have to scold me. I have to correct me. I have to congratulation me. I have to discipline me. I have to grade me. I have to examine me. I have to kick myself in my own ass to make sure that I achieve what the fuck it is I want to achieve. No questions. No talk. Get busy and stay busy. Get focused and stay focused.

My best days are still yet to come.

Monday, January 1, 2019

We still focused and our aim is intact. The plan has been put together and we are now merely executing what we've already laid down on paper. The progress not swift but steady and that's all we want and need. No need to rush anything as time is our ally and friend.

I accept my setbacks and adversity, whether self-manufactured or from external sources, as necessary education and training to get me where I want to go. The pain hurts. It usually lasts 24-48 hours *(that's as long as I'll tolerate it before I change my polarity and come up out that shit)*. However, as the pain subsides, it motivates me even more than before.

Renewed and refreshed with new experiences, I am now even more prepared to succeed. I continue to exercise daily, eat clean foods daily and get my proper sleep daily. As long as I do this I am ahead of the game and the masses of other people who are not so disciplined.

Money!

Sunday, February 24, 2019

I haven't written in a while. Almost 2 months. I've been super super busy and focused on my YouTube Channel which has seen tremendous growth in the last 4 months. I've expanded the scope of my content to include fitness training, motivation, interviews and expressing my views about current events. I've gotten some coffee mugs made up with my book on them (Volume I) and I'm gearing up to get some T-Shirts made up as well. I just ordered some more books to sell and I'm going to really go hard with selling my books as this will translate into more subscribers for the YouTube Channel and more money for me.

I was disheartened initially when the book didn't sell as "I expected" it to and turned that inward against myself and got disinterested in even attempting to sell my book. I viewed the weak sales as the entire world rejecting my writing. I thought this into reality in my own dome. How the fuck could that be stupid ass Nigga. If the whole world read your book then you would've had way more sales than what you have had thus far.

I still see how easy it is for me to "go against me" at any moment. However, "understanding is one of the best things in the world". Now I know and understand fully when I start with that sucka-shit of "going against me" and I immediately remedy and rectify the situation. I do this by reversing the polarity of my mind and focus on the tile opposite of "going against me" and begin to "root for me", "celebrate me", "cheer for me". Then I'm cured.

I am going to go hard as a muthaphucka with selling my books and T-shirts.

I'm in the process of creating a website "retail store" for my books, coffee mugs and T-shirts. I'm going to incorporate some interactive media on the site and make it look real nice. I'm focused and determined to find a glorious end.

I got it!

Friday, March 01, 2019

Ordered more books to sell both Volume I's and Volume II's. I'm going to go after it with renewed energy and focus on this go around. The last batch that I ordered and sold previously, I was not "on top of my sales game" and actually not confident in my material that I was selling. That is over with. I'm back and I'm going to go all out and push to move these books so that I can order more and keep selling and augment my financial position to get me where I want to go.

I have to admit that I need a significant amount of money in order to do what I really want to do and fulfill my dreams. There is nothing wrong with this you see as in this world of 2019, in order for me to actualize my vision it is imperative that I get on my "money-making" game. I have been on it don't get me wrong, however, since coming out of prison 3 years ago, my mindset towards money has been 11,000% transmuted from what it used to be, how I looked at it, what I was willing to do to acquire it and how I used it. I have a completely different perspective on my views of money and it's importance in my life.

When I got out the joint, I fully understood that true wealth and true happiness are within the mind and are more tied to:

- Peace of mind
- Spiritual cleanliness
- Top notch physical conditioning
- Sufficient rest and sleep

- The absence of problems
- Keeping the number of my affairs to a minimum

I understand that if I have these and have no currency in my pocket that I am still very rich. The aforementioned bullet points are in conjunction with the health of my Sun and closest family members of course.

I made $1,000,000 before and I am going to do it again. I have a reference point of having done it already. I have a variety of products in place that will aide me in getting there. I have a will "inside" of me that is unmatched on this planet. I haven't met anyone with more drive than I do. I see mediocre people every day acquiring wealth however they do, so this lets me know that it is inevitable that I will again. I will not be outdone by anyone. My story will be told for years to come about how you can get to the top...crash and burn....and rise anew to even higher heights than the first time. I will show and prove.

It's my turn to win. I am in tremendous physical shape so the energy is there. I got it!

Self-Confrontation Is A Must And Continual

The more I live the more I see that my greatest enemy and my most dangerous battles in my life have been with and against myself. Even after doing extensive internal work on myself, examining myself and truly rectifying my defects, it never fails that time will pass and I will look up only to find that some character flaw that I thought I eradicated has re-emerged and resurfaced again in an attempt to zap my enthusiasm, belief, self-confidence and destroy me.

My reaction to this is one of two ways. Either I immediately recognize it, acknowledge it, dissect it, ask myself what's wrong and penetrate to the core of the issue and get rid of it immediately or I run away and try to act like its not there which begins the steep decline to low self-esteem and self-hatred. Fortunately, I am fully aware of this and I have a very good understanding of myself to know and be cognizant of what I am doing and what I need to do in order to "get Right".

The key is to stand and fight.

Thursday, March 07, 2019

In spite of mental fatigue, I have to continue to press forward and execute my plan in order to reach my destination.

Tuesday, June 04, 2019

I have to do better. I have to do better than what I have been doing. My performance is not up to my potential. I should be further along than where I am. I have been underperforming in my own life. My performance has been substandard. I give myself a grade of C thus far.

My focus needs to change and I am going to change it. My attention needs to shift and I will shift it. My concentration needs adjustment and it will get adjusted. My discipline needs to be tightened up and I am going to tighten it. My rest and sleep needs improving (this is my treasure) and I am going to get back on my rest and sleep game something heavy. I will withdraw from the world until I get myself where I want to be (this is required for goal achievement). I should be further along than where I am at this moment and I don't have any excuses for myself other than I am massively underperforming.

I know how to get there. I have prepared for this. I have been there so I know I can go again. I have done it before and will do it again. This time will be sweeter though. This time will be more exciting. This time will be deeper and more fulfilling. This time will cap off the story and cement my legacy in the hearts of My Sun's grandchildren and all the posterity to follow.

Friday, June 07, 2019

It's time to go ahead and do what I need to do to get to where I'm going. I'm ready. Enough is enough. The time is now. I have what it takes already in my possession. It is doable and I'm going to do it. It can't be impossible because I see lesser people there. Nothing is impossible!

Gotta stay even keel though. Don't get too high on the successes and wins and don't get too low on the losses and temporary defeats. Gotta be damn near "dead & emotionless" and just knowing that with consistency it must come to me.

Don't look to the left at him - don't look to the right at them and begin to concern myself with what they are doing. Just focus on my game! My game is the best right now even though I am not where I think I should be. I see lesser people in more exposed and prominent positions and I get frustrated knowing that I have more substance to offer than they ever could.

I due time.

Tuesday, June 11, 2019

I'm motivated and back focused like I should be. My YouTube channel consumes me at times and gets me off my "center" and I forget briefly all of the progress I have made thus far since getting out of prison. However, when I look at where I am versus where I was or could've been I am doing an excellent job living my life.

My financial success is slow in coming but I know it's on the way. All I need is that "one exposure moment" and I'm gone! Because the way I see it there is nobody out here telling a story like mines if there is even a story like mines to tell. I see lesser people in positions of exposure with absolutely nothing to offer other than conformity, assimilation, compromise and buffoonery. It frustrates me to see this when I know I'm so much better yet unknown. I will change this and when the world meets me I will show them someone unlike anyone they've seen before.

Friday, June 21, 2019

Be like a "rubber ball" and bounce back. Bounce back in every aspect of the word or thought. Spiritually then mentally... once you do these 2 the physical takes care of itself and is a byproduct of both. Taking me time. Slowing my mind down and reminding myself not to rush. I was talking to a 76-year old guy Tuesday and he told me....

"I ain't in a rush to do nuthin'"....

That was profound to me because to have live as long as he has and for him to say that ...he must "know sumthin'". I then immediately thought about my life in its "current state" and said to myself... How can you apply that to your life right now Sean? How can what you just heard benefit you?

If I'm going to "get on" I have to "put myself on". Nobody is coming to help me "put me on". If it's going to happen then I have to do it for myself. I can and I will.

Things take time to develop, sprout and grow. The key is slowing my mind down to fully understand and appreciate that and not get down and frustrated when things take longer than what I want, expect and thinks should happen. My job is just to keep getting up everyday writing, filming, editing, reading, working out, saving my money and putting in the footwork to effect my destiny in my life.

Nobody is coming to help you. You have to help yourself Sean.

THE NEXT PARAGRAPH IS MY 1ST TIME WRITING IN 8 MONTHS.......

Saturday, April 4, 2020

I haven't written in a long while as you can see from the previous date. My writing style is such that I have to "feel" like writing. I have to be "moved" to write. I never force myself to write a book or any document that I'm writing from my soul.

A lot has changed since I last wrote. My YouTube Channel has grown immensely and continues to grow every day. I now have a solid pack of 45,000 Subscribers. I recently sold my window cleaning business and am now transitioning and moving upward to my next Chapter in my life experience. I am putting together a "Motivational Speaker" conference featuring some other YouTubers that is going to "change the game" and open up more opportunities for them and me as well.

Lil Sean is doing great which is to be expected as he has the best and "Dopest Father On The Planet". He is getting ready to complete the 3rd grade, growing taller everyday and developing his own personality. I love it. Whenever he is here at home, I make him do "10 Sets of 10's" on Push Ups and Body Squats, we eat clean and talk strong powerful conversations about "mental toughness and being in control of our destiny". He is 8 years old.

I am back trading in the market more regularly and having success. I have losing days and winning days. I need both in order to grow and get better.

I just turned 51 Yrs and I feel excellent, fit and Strong. I am still in tremendous condition all around the board... Spiritually, Mentally and Physically. I still train no less than 5 days a week "YEAR ROUND" and I have no gym membership. All of my training is done inside the crib or outside in the park no matter how fuckin' cold it is. I GOTTA GIT MINE!!!

My life is interesting right now at this point in time. I have no idea where it's headed but I do know it's headed somewhere good and better than where I've ever been because I'm doing the footwork and it all POSITIVE. So even though I don't know where I will end up ... I do know it will be in a good place because I'm doing all "Right and Positive" moves, with all "Right and Positive" thoughts, putting forth "Right and Positive" vibrations, operating on "Right and Positive" frequencies and wave lengths and I got my muthaphuckin head to the sky!!!!!

Peace out

Later that night………………………………………..

Today was an awesome day. Worked out 2x today, ate clean, got a couple of orders for books and T-Shirts but more importantly I've started back to write. It feels good. The time is now for the Brutha to "git back on my game"….. Focused, Determined, Tenacious, Impetuous and Relentless. Gotta envision and create the "super ending" cementing my legacy.

The time is now.

Sunday, April 5, 2020

Up and at 'em again this morning. Just got finished running about 2 miles up at the park and now gittin' ready to make me some breakfast. Late night bootie call last night got a me a little sluggish today but you know what we do. We shake dat shit off and keep pushin' forward no matter what.

Everything is on lockdown and closed right now due to the CORONAVIRUS PANDEMIC (if it even exists?) so the whole planet is on crash. The news media incessantly bombards the viewers with "repeated and looped images" of depressing and deflating news. I don't watch any of it. I'm not interested in what they have to say at all. I stay focused on my plan and continue to execute while there is down time in the country so as soon as it opens back up ...I got a head start.

My brand and YouTube Channel are growing exponentially due to the amount of hard work, consistency and dedication I am putting into it. It amazes me as to what this "Brand & YouTube Channel" have become. I never imagined this and it was not apart of my plan when I shot my 1st video. When I shot that 1st video I was after MONEY. It was to promote my 1st book (Volume I) and generate sales. 2 years and some change later it has morphed into something much more than that. I am still in it for the MONEY absolutely, however, it seems as though my SUBSCRIBERS have chosen me to save lives.

I get DM's (direct messages) on all my social media platforms from people all over the world telling me how my videos and story has touched their individual lives. How my videos and content motivate them to push forward in their own life. Recently, I've had someone tell me that my videos stopped them from killing themselves. WOW.......WOW!!!! I never foresaw this...but now that I'm here I'm cool wit it.

I will continue to move forward and I will never "let up on my set up". My best days are in front of me.

Friday, April 10, 2020

Things are good. I sold my window cleaning business, all my bills are paid, there is food in the refrigerator, Lil Sean is strong and healthy, I am healthy, I look good and my future success is assured. I will not be denied.

Washed clothes today (well I took them to the laundromat for the lady to wash them), edited some videos, shot some videos, edited some more videos and now I'm waiting on Lil Sean to come home. Everything is good. I don't have any complaints. This CORONAVIRUS lockdown has altered my life temporarily (I think) and has brought the entire world to a standstill. It's a very interesting time to be alive and see this NEW WORLD ORDER unfolding before my eyes. THE ENTIRE PLANET HAS BEEN STOPPED IN IT'S TRACKS..... shit is incredible.

Given that, I still remain spiritually and mentally fit and strong and I stay ready. I will capitalize on this situation and make it work for me. I refuse to get bogged down with the television (TEL – LIE – VISION) reports and misinformation and let that stagnate me into non-action. I remain focused on what I am doing and on my Master Plan.

I have a big project that I'm currently working on and was working on prior to this CORONAVIRUS outbreak that is going to be historic and epic. It's something that has never been done before and will be a game changer all over the world. This is will be one of the many things I will be remembered for and this will be another rung on my Legacy Ladder. I am so looking forward to seeing it unfold. You will know what I am speaking of when you read this part of the book now.

Be True…………Be Bold……………Be Aggressive!

Tuesday, April 14, 2020

The YouTube Channel is growing every day. I'm selling books and T-Shirts here and there and that helps too. I sold my window cleaning business so at this moment in time… I am a Full Time YouTuber and Options Trader. It's amazing when I think of how much my life has changed for the better inside of 4 years (since being released from Federal Prison) and 2 years (started my YouTube Channel in January 2018). It's been a journey and I have persevered to my advantage. The best is yet to come.

I am prepared for whatever happens and whatever comes my way. I have done the work. I have done the internal work. I have done the mental work of "numbing" my mind to anything I choose at any moment. I have done the physical work of maintaining my body to be fight ready at any moment. This was all necessary. And you know what's crazy??? The place that society says is so bad, negative and horrible and a place that I was scared to go to and was trying at all cost to avoid is where…….. I LAID THIS FOUNDATION. Yeap… Federal Prison (Federal Correctional Institution Morgantown, Morgantown, West Virginia).

Who knew? I had no idea. I stayed out and fought my case for 3.5 years until finally I said "FUCK IT" let me go git this shit over wit." Now upon reflection, I went to FCI Morgantown at precisely the right time to be incarcerated with the dudes I was there with and at just the right time. I met some dudes in there that HELPED ME FIX ME. Dudes I was close too and dudes that I was not close to that did not like me and I did not like them. (YEAP even they taught me and HELPED me).

This shit is amazing.

My life is the shit!

Thursday, June 18, 2020

Mistakes have to be "put to use" to aide me on the next go around. Mistakes are not to be lamented for long lengths of time ultimately driving my thoughts and life into the ground. Mistakes are not meant to make me forever regret them and perpetually live in the past wondering how I ever made the mistake in the first place being that I AM MR. PERFECT. No….. No….. No……

That's not how this shit go…..

Mistakes are to used to strengthen my resolve and be the impetus or driving force for my "next try", because ain't no way I'm givin' up on me. Mistakes are for me to reflect, take myself to task and ask myself some tough tough questions about "Who am I?".. "What happened?"…… How did it happen? What part did I play in it? Where did I fuck up at? What could have I done to prevent me fucking up the way I did? And LASTLY….. How do I learn from the mistake and prevent its reoccurrence? This is what mistakes are for. They are to be used to bring about a more rigorous application of my focus, determination and drive. I am to learn from them. They are there so that I may learn and grow. Yes growth comes from the pain of making mistakes.

"If it don't hurt … you ain't learnt nuthin'….."

my Bunkie in prison said this to me one day while we were debating some issue or two.

I just made another mistake this week in the stock market where I took a HUGE loss that was easily preventable had I accepted early on that I was on the WRONG side of the trade. Got out of that trade and got on the RIGHT side of the trade. But hey… It didn't go that way …….. but that's cool…. Because what valuable information that I did gain was that I know that I can "run my account up" to $100,000. I know for a fact I can. And that's just what I'm finna do starting today. So I'm cool. I'm super cool because I don't have no pressure of time constraints nor am I trading with "desperate capital" so with that being said……

I am prepared. I prepared for this in FCI Morgantown. I prepared for just this event in front of me. I've done the homework, I've done the internal work, I've done the discipline work, I've done the mental work, I'm physically fit so that means AIN'T NUTHIN' CAN STOP ME…………………but ME. And I ain't finna do that because I have a love affair goin' on with me now….

Saturday, June 27, 2020

"Setbacks" and "things not working out as you planned them" is a part of the game that must be mastered in order to keep movin' forward. It must be understood internally that it is ok for your plans to be delayed as a result of a setback, however, that does not mean you abandon your map, plan or yourself as a result. The setback must be put into proper perspective and understood that that is all it is "a setback" and not a signal to quit.

The vision in your mind must be matched up with your heart and you must tell yourself and know that that vision will exist one day, that it will be a reality in this life. It is lonely on this path and you will be all by your muthaphuckin' self……….and that's cool and definitely necessary because no one is can see your "inner vision" as it's inside of you and it's yours. In fact, nobody cares that you have a vision while it's inside of you, they will only come to care and be attracted to you once its manifested in the physical form…..

Piece of shit muthaphuckas…………………….. lolololololol

But don't be discouraged or upset as this is only human nature and it too is apart of the process. The main focus is that you do not get too emotional and allow yourself to become paralyzed with disappointment. Everything must be kept in its right perspective and looked at as nothing more than "life happening" in real time. This must be mastered mentally. This is super important.

Sunday, November 08, 2020

Good Morning!!

It's been a psychologically challenging last 3 weeks since my mother died. My mother's death in and of itself was not the toughest part. Although I miss my mother my soul is at peace because I know she lived a "full" life of 77 years, was never a burden to anyone up until her last days and he really loved my son, Sean X. Gunby Jr. My son and her had developed a relationship that was a true as can be.

The part that was the most fucked up was my mother's son, brother, nephews and nieces lining up against her and stealing a lot of her personal belongings while she lay dead in the funeral home. This is the part that made the whole situation mentally stressful and disheartening.

The attorney with whom she had drafter her last "Will" with began to communicate directly with my mother's brother and nieces about the content and language of the will (utter violation of attorney-client privilege) and refused to talk to me. I began to hear rumors about what was in the Will and that she had purportedly left everything to Lil Sean. Nonetheless, the Will has now somehow come up missing and can't be found. This shit is crazy. This was a true punch in the mouth and something that I could have never expected but this shit is REAL.

I had initially made up my mind to just say fuck everything and turn my back on the entire situation and just walk away from it and let it do what it was gonna do. But I have since changed my mind and I'm going to get involved with my mother's stuff and make sure that Lil Sean gets all that she wanted him to have. This is going to be a slight distraction and take away from my YouTube Channel but it's something that has to get done.

Sometimes life is going to blind-side the shit outta you through no fault of your own and throw your life into disarray. This is part of the game. But when it happens you have to dig in and "git down for your crown" and go all out and assert yourself as a force to be reckoned with. Everyone and everything has to faced head on and all challenges and challengers met with a force like they've never seen before. Fuck 'em. Fuck 'em all. You can't let weak, snake-like muthaphuckas take advantage of you and move you. You must impose your will upon them, especially if you are in the right. This shit don't never stop!

Saturday, December 05, 2020

Good Morning!!

It's time to start writing again. For me writing is therapeutic. It is my medicine. After I write (express myself) I always feel better. Even when I confront situations and express myself verbally with words I feel 100x lighter. For me to "hold inside" my thoughts and feelings with attempts to conceal them from the world, but even worse, try to hide them from myself, is to "weight myself down" mentally and spiritually which inevitably leads to physical lethargy and lack of energy and motivation.

This past 7 weeks for me since my Mom Dukes past away have been super weird to say the least. Not only did my Mom Dukes pass away so abruptly which fucked me up in and of itself, but then my family acted like savages and buzzards and went in her house and stole all her personal belongings (Honda & Mercedes Benz car keys, diamond jewelry, gold jewelry, THE WILL, checkbooks, titles to the cars, bible, clothes and who the fuck knows what else).

About 7 months ago, out of the blue, my Mother called me and told me that she left a WILL with an attorney in Washington, Georgia named MV Booker. This was extremely shocking to me because my Mother was a very private person and played her cards close to the vest. Four months later she called me again and told me that she was going to the dentist to have a tooth procedure and that "if it go left I left my WILL with Ms. Booker". I said ok.

The day after my Mother died, October 23, 2020, I began calling Ms. Booker to obtain THE WILL. No answer. 17 calls from both my Mother's cell phone and my cell phone. No answer. I sent text messages. No reply. I went to her office and left messages with people that I was looking for her. No call back. I went to her personal residence. No answer. This attorney has still not contacted me to this day. However, she has been in regular contact with my other family members who went in my house and stole from my Mother.

I have heard from 3 different people (family members) with direct knowledge that my Mother's WILL left everything to Lil Sean (Sean X. Gunby Jr.), my son.

THIS SHIT IS CRAZY!!!

(smile…… because that's all that keeps me calm right now)

Nonetheless, I continue to pay my Mothers mortgages and take care of her personal business. I continue to remain true to her wishes and I'm ready to fight to the death if need be.

Peace out

Sean G

Sunday, December 06, 2020

We still movin' forward. Shit ain't goin' like I want it to go or as I know it should go, but I still got to keep moving forward. When tough times come they come in a big way and it's usually a few things all at the same time. I'm keeping my poise and at this stage of the game I have understanding that things do pass. All I have to do is keep my cool and keep doing the right things for the right reasons EVEN IF IT DON'T FEEL GOOD.

I was chillin'……. My life was on point and then all of a sudden out of the blue life punched me square in my mouth through no fault of my own. That's cool. This shit don't feel good at all but I'mma handle it. I GOT IT!!

Monday, December 07, 2020

Today was a successful day. Got a lot of shit done today. A lot of paperwork that needed to be done, phone calls that needed to be made, books, shirts and hats shipped out and meetings attended. Worked out. Did "10 Sets of 26's" on Push Ups, ate clean and minded my business. Uploaded videos to YouTube. Fed Lil Sean good food and helped him with his schoolwork.

What a difference a day makes.

Today was alright.

Wednesday, December 09, 2020

This Shit Don't Stop!!!

You gotta go deep to find out who you are. What you love. What you hate. What you fear. What gets you high. What floats your boat. To truly learn the essence of who you are you gotta be able to go DEEP. You gotta be brave. You gotta be courageous. You gotta be fearless. You gotta be true. You gotta be bold. You gotta be aggressive. This ain't no job for little boys. This ain't no job for lil girls. This a job for MEN. This a job for WOMEN. Get ready for the git ready. Get ready to feel every emotion there is to feel and fight through the fear. If you can do this you will find GOLD & TREASURES on the other side.

Thursday, December 10, 2020

KEEP APPLYING THE PRESSURE.........TO YOURSELF!

Never let up in asking more of yourself. Never allow yourself to get mentally comfortable with your progress or performance thus far. Demand even more accuracy from yourself. Demand more vigilance from yourself. Force yourself to be more dedicated, determined and resolved to winning convincingly. Never get comfortable with where you are at.

So What!! You made it.

Fuck dat. Keep pushing for more. You can become greater than this. There is more potential locked inside of you that you need to dig deep in order to get it out. Go there. Go inside yourself with your shovel and flashlight and DIG, DIG, DIG, DIG DEEPER to get what is inherently and intrinsically yours. Stop fucking around with bullshit and bullshit people. Fuck them muthaphuckas. They ain't got no dreams, they ain't got no aim, they ain't got no vision….they "lost in the sauce"…."stuck like Chuck"…. And as long as you keep hanging with them and giving them airplay on your frequency waves…. YOU WILL STAY STUCK WITH THEM…..

DON'T LET UP ON YA SET UP!!!

\///

REGROUP & COMEBACK ON 'EM!!

Just because you suffered a setback "today" don't mean you can't comeback tomorrow. All you gotta do is "regroup" and try again. Look at what you did wrong. Look at who you had around you. Look at what went wrong. Look at what you could've done differently. Look at who you trusted that fronted on you. Look at why you trusted them. Look at why you didn't see the signs that they wasn't shit. Look at why you ignored those signs. Look at why you chose them to be in your arena in the first place. What is or was it about you then that chose and allowed weaklings to get close to you. Look at what part you played. Ask yourself why.

This takes courage.

Sean G

Monday, January 4, 2021

BE DETERMINED ---- SEE IT THROUGH TIL THE END

A determined mind is unconquerable and doesn't even consider failure or not achieving a vision. A determined mindset ain't thinking about no bullshit....ain't wastin' no time with petty games and people....ain't even conversating with aimless people and sees everything that happens as a "next step" in getting to where he/she wants to go. Even if the "next step" is super fucked-up and has occurred through no fault of his own. You see this mindset..... (THE DETERMINED MINDSET) ...... is poised for accomplishment because it can already see the accomplishment beforehand.

A DETERMINED MINDSET can see the future because it will create its future through hard work and dedication. This mindset don't play no games, don't fuck around and doesn't appreciate you coming to it with bullshit, fuckery and baffoonery. Why is the mindset so coarse, insensitive and very matter-of-fact.

I will tell you why..................... Read and listen carefully

It don't give a fuck what you think because its got something to do. What you think has no bearing on it because it knows that (IT AND ONLY IT) will get the dream realized. It's not concerned with your opinion because the plan has already been written, mapped out and is being executed as we speak. So what you got to say ain't even important and you just wastin' your breathe and time trying to persuade or convince THE DETERMINED MINDSET otherwise.

You see this DETERMINED MINDSET has already been through so much shit, self-manufactured and brought on by suckas, that it has not feelings or emotions anymore. At this point its all mathematics and science, everything will add up and the science of the plan will play out just the way science manifests and plays out in nature and The Universe.

So leave me the fuck alone………………..

I'M DETERMINED TO WIN!

Peace out

Sean G

Monday, January 11, 2021

You gotta be able to stand on your own 2 feet. You gotta be able to stand alone by yourself. You gotta be able to be comfortable in your truth. This makes all the difference in the world. There are many people who "appear" to have it all together on the exterior or on the outside but inside they are fucked up, untrue, insecure and plastic. They prop themselves up with material things such as cars, clothes, jewelry, etc., but if you were to "lift up the hood" and check "behind the curtain" you will see them a very shaky, insecure and fright filled person.

I do not want to be as such.

It's much more comfortable to be solid, firm and true. To have "my outside matching my inside". To know that I am SOLID to the core. This means most to me. Fuck all that other shit. I spent a lot of time in my youth years "trying to act as if" and "be what I thought another muthaphuckka would like"……….. Man FUCK DAT SHIT… That's an utter and complete waste of time and so psychologically damaging and uncomfortable. In the end it called ……………SOUL SUICIDE.

Tuesday, January 12, 2021

We can start over anytime we want. You can "start your life over" whenever you get ready. All of you have to do is make the decision or decisions. This is totally up to you. You can renew your mind upon your request. All you have to do is make the decision that "I am going to do this" and set about the task of making the changes necessary to bring about your new life.

You WILL have to cut some people off. You WILL have to change those behaviors that are no longer useful or conducive to you new way of life. You WILL have to form new habits and thought processes that coalesce more harmoniously with your new way of living. A lot of changes WILL have to be made but nonetheless they can made and YOU CAN CHANGE YOUR LIFE.

Wednesday, January 13, 2021

Another successful day down. Tomorrow will be a repeat of today. Tomorrow will be another successful day because I will make it one. I have the power to effect my hours, days, weeks, months, years, life and DESTINY!

Thursday, January 14, 2021

Chillin' here in the crib BY MYSELF! And …… It's ALRIGHTTTTT. It feels good. It's super quiet. I don't have no music on. I don't have no TV on. I don't have nuthin' on. It's total silence. The only thing I hear right now is the keys from this keyboard "poppin'" as I type this book and the sound of my fish tank filter running the water into the tank.

PEACE OF MIND

There is nothing like it. I don't care where you go, whatchu buy, whatchu eat, where you live, how much money you have, how much pussy you git, how many cars you have, what kind of car you have, what kind of jewelry you have, how big your house is, how many house you got, how much money you make, how much money you have…. You name it……. Ain't nuthin' like

PEACE OF MIND

I can clearly remember as if it were 17 minutes ago, when I was serving my time in Federal Prison (FCI Morgantown, Morgantown, West Virginia) at it "came over me" and I finally realized that **PEACE OF MIND** was king. That all that I had been looking for in the pussy, the money, the cars, the clothes, the bullshit…. was never to be found there in those things. I had discovered that what I had been searching for my whole life was in abundance in **PEACE OF MIND**. I was finally able to mentally rest. I was finally able to exhale, breathe and let out a sigh of relief that I no longer had to search outside of myself for what I wanted or needed but all I had to do was look inward…..within and inside of myself and there it was. Riches, treasures, happiness like I had never ever seen before and it was called

PEACE OF MIND

I clearly remember talkin' to different dudes in the joint from drug dealers, killers, doctors, senators, politicians, gun possession, drug kingpins, CEO's, stock brokers, mortgage brokers, etc., etc..
We would talk for hours, days, weeks and months about their case, my case, their lives before prison, my life before prison, wild shit they did, crazy shit I did, how they got busted, how I got busted and on and on and on.
And after we got done telling the war stories the overruling theme, thought and realization from EVERY SINGLE person I spoke to….was that they hadn't experienced the level of **PEACE OF MIND** that they had experienced since they got locked up. And they spoke of the **PEACE OF MIND** in a utopian experience and loved the effervescence that this **PEACE OF MIND** brought to them.

A lot of these dudes had been hundred thousandaires, millionaires and multi-millionaires (some still were…not everybody was broke like me) but they didn't miss the money as much as they enjoyed having **PEACE OF MIND**. This was a "spiritual awakening" for me because I thought it was only me that felt this way. I was mistaken. They all had discovered something way more valuable than money, pussy or things…….. and it was….. **PEACE OF MIND**.

A lot of them thanked their prison experience for this epiphany and vowed to always choose **PEACE OF MIND** over any of that other bullshit that we had been led to believe meant something. We had discovered that that other shit (pussy, cars, money, houses, clothes) was fuckin' meaningless in the grand scheme of things.

Yes. This is a true story

PEACE OF MIND

Monday, January 18, 2021

In spite of all the distractions, buffoonery, fuckery and noise going on around me....I still stay STEADY EDDIE. I don't alter my thought process from the goals I have set for myself. I don't allow myself to get caught up in the bullshit going on around me. I watch, see, listen and observe but I don't let it impact my plans to the point where I get stagnated and stuck. Of course I will make adjustments and adaptations if need be but for the "here and now" I remain focused on my mission and my mission is to keep winning.

Tuesday, January 19, 2021

We are up and we are at 'em! I'm up and I'm at 'em. I'm in motion in spite of the what's going on in the world today and even in my life. I feel tremendous sadness, regret and anger surrounding the events of my mothers death and everybody who was involved, but some way somehow I am going to have to "get that behind me" and move forward knowing that I acted right, behaved as I should have and did the right thing on mines and Lil Sean's part.

Sometimes I feel like I could have done more to prevent the thieves from doing what they did but I couldn't. There is no way for me to have known what was going to take place because your mother dies only once. There is no trial run, no rehearsal and no practice. It's all live and in action. No need to look back at what would've, could've, should've, wishing and hoping. It's over and what has been done is done. I gotta figure out a way to move forward from what "should have happened" and "what my mother wanted to happen" from what actually happened. That's the key. So far I haven't been able to do it. But one day I will.

++

HOW YOU CAN KNOW WHO WILL WIN....

Who can persevere the best? Who can endure the most? Who can last the longest? Who can overcome mental fatigue more often? Who can fight through the pain? Who can harness the pain and make it work for them? Who can keep goin' when don't nobody else want to keep goin'? Who can flip the switch and go completely emotionless? Who can see the end goal in sight no matter how dark it is? Who makes the most of their free time to plan, prepare, get ready and stay ready? Who can center their spirit in the midst of chaos? Who can maintain their discipline and keep to it like muthaphuckka when it is super imperative to?

Who can stand alone when standing on their beliefs and convictions without giving a fuck what another muthaphuckka think? Who keeps it true to themselves? Who stays loyal to himself/herself? Who remains steadfast and committed to his purpose? Who understand the importance of time wasted? Who understand the value of time utilized? Who understand that his/her time here on this plane of existence is finite and limited and knowing this does not fuck around with bullshit? Who is brave when necessary? Who is courageous when necessary? Who is violent when necessary? Who is courageous when necessary? Who is aggressive when necessary? Who is peaceful with necessary? Who is passive when necessary? Who understands himself to the depths of his being? Who knows himself completely? Who is his best friend? Who has a love affair with himself? Who has true and complete knowledge of self? Who accepts himself on the deepest level? Who approves of himself irrespective of how anyone else may feel?

Who loves himself?

THIS IS HOW YOU CAN KNOW WHO WILL WIN...

Thursday, January 21, 2021

Still on the case like a well paid attorney with 1 client. Gotta remain vigilant and not get caught up and distracted by the noise in the media, in the country, in my state, in my city, in my neighborhood, in my family and in my house. Gotta stay focused. Gotta keep believing in the "possible" and working toward it every day.

Monday, January 25, 2021

Stay tough. Stay tough. Stay mentally cold. Stay ready. Stay aware of everything that is happening. Stay observant. Keep your eyes and ears open. Don't take nothing with a minimum of concern. Take everything at FACE VALUE. Respond to what is...... not what you want it to be. Don't get emotional. Understand that this is your life and that you have to live with you. This is very important because things affect our self-perception, self-esteem and self-respect and we have to make sure that these are always maintained on a high level even if we have to take a loss in other ways.

Stay tough......

Friday, January 29, 2021

Good Morning.... Another day that gets me closer to my vision. Another day that gets me closer to my dream. Another day that gets me closer to my goals. I take advantage of this shit. I don't let one day get past me without me squeezing everything I can outta that muthaphuckka. I don't work for the day .... I make the day work for me. I use the 86,400 seconds I am afforded by The Sun, The Moon and The Stars to "make hay while the Sun shines".

It's my responsibility to make whatever I want to happen to happen. Nobody else is obligated to cheer me on, assist me, help me, encourage me, root for me, advise me......none of that shit. THIS SHIT IS ALL ON ME!!!

I GOT IT!!

Sean G

February 4, 2021

INTEGRITY IS A MUST

Integrity is super important. It is your "instant report card" to yourself. You can't front of your lack of integrity. It will haunt you if you don't have it. It is clearly visible immediately upon you opening your mouth whether you have INTEGRITY or not.

Not having it will get you barred from places. Having it will get your FREE ADMISSION to many places. Not having it will leave you lonely. Having it will keep you content. Not having it will get you shunned by those that have it. Having it will make you magnetic.

You gotta have integrity (strict personal honesty). If you are working out alone and you said you were going to do 10 Sets of 10's then you can't do 9 Sets or 9 reps on the 10th set. You have to do all that shit EVEN WHEN AIN'T NOBODY LOOKING.

February 6, 2021

STAY IN MOTION

Don't never stop movin' on your life. Don't never stop laying down the foundation. Don't never stop setting up the foundational blocks. Don't never stop pouring the concrete on your life. Don't never stop gittin' shit together. Keep your game tight. Keep your shit in order. Stay on top of your game. Fuck all the bullshit. That shit is a waste of mental energy you must always remember this part. Keep the focus on your life and your vision and fuck all the "noise" goin' on around you. Fuck dat shit. That shit don't mean nuthin'. Just keep moving forward.

February 17, 2021

YOU ARE GOING TO HAVE TO TAKE SOME CHANCES

In order to grow from where you are you are going to have to take some chances and take on some sort of risk. You can't play it safe all the time if you are trying to achieve your vision. Your dream is your dream and in order for you to achieve such you are going to have to move out of your comfort zone, break from your usual train of thought and take a chance. This is the only way you will get there.

You will have to "go it alone" most times and you will be by yourself while you are in the middle of achieving your DEFINITE CHIEF AIM and making your world what you want it to be. Nobody is going to take your chances for you or with you because they will not want to share is your stress, failure or defeat. However, when you succeed (because you will) they will most definitely want to share in your joy, success and victory. GUARANTEED. But this doesn't matter, you still have to make it happen and you can as long as you put in the footwork, be patient, diligent and focused on your end result.

Stay on top of your game, be aggressive and move forward with confidence.

March 6, 2021

PERSEVERE

In spite of the obstacles keep moving forward. In spite of the adversity keep moving forward. In spite of the betrayal keep moving forward. In spite of the broken promises keep moving forward. In spite of the backstabbing keep moving forward. In spite of the nonsense keep moving forward. In spite of the self-doubt keep moving forward. In spite of the bullshit……KEEP MOVING FORWARD.

There will be times when this is all you have to tell yourself. Everything will be fucked up, out of shape and in disarray and it will appear that you are "stuck like Chuck" and not making any progress. You will begin to question whatever it is that you are doing and your ability to achieve that goal, dream or vision. You will be all alone and all you will be able to tell yourself is……….

JUST KEEP MOVING FORWARD……….. **PERSEVERE!**

Friday, March 12, 2021

HAPPY BIRTHDAY TO ME

I turned 52 years old yesterday and I feel great. Life moves on and on and on and on and on. It doesn't stop. The older I get the better I get. I am in tremendous spiritual, mental and physical health and I appear to be getting stronger and stronger with each passing day. I have a good life. I love my life.

I accept my life and myself with all it's ups and downs as I understand that "everything that is in the Universe is inside of me" and as there are storms, hurricanes, tornadoes, blizzards, rain, calm, sun, clouds, sunlight, clear skies, gorgeous clouds and beautiful rays of Sun….my life will mirror this because I am one with The Universe. There is no disconnection between us (The Universe and I) as we are both bound up together as one and can never be without each other.

Saturday, March 13, 2021

Keep the pressure on yourself to keep getting better, to be more disciplined, to be more focused and the see your plan through to the end. Keep doing all of the necessary things you need to do to make your dream a reality. Don't be indulging in bullshit, conversating with bullshit people, being distracted by bullshit encounters or entertaining any kind of bullshit no matter where it comes from. Keep on top of ya game. Keep your spirit clean. Keep your heart clean. Keep your mind clean. Keep your body clean.

KEEP THE PRESSURE SQARELY ON YaSELF….FUCK EVERYBODY ELSE.

Thursday, March 18, 2021

We don't stop no matter what. That ain't got nuthin' to do with what I'm doing? I can't get bogged down listening to that nonsense. I can't get sidetracked by the chaos in other peoples lives. I know it sounds fucked up but I can't. It's too expensive. My time ain't to be wasted because can't nobody reimburse me for my time lost on bullshit. Therefore, I don't partake in bullshit. I don't fuck wit people who bullshit around. I don't listen to muthaphuckkas who talk bullshit. I don't hang around people who entertain bullshit. I ain't got time for no bullshit.

I GOTTA MAKE DIS SHIT HAPPEN WHILE I'M YOUNG, GOT MY ENERGY, MY DRIVE AND MY MUTHAPHUCKKIN' LIFE.

Yes sir baby. The time is now not tomorrow. I'm gonna die one day and I'll be just a memory to all you muthaphuckkas and that's ok. However, I will have at least done my thing, made my COMEBACK and fulfilled my vision while I was here in this muthaphuckka. And MOST IMPORTANTLY, I will leave a legacy engraved in the minds, hearts and souls of my posterity for generations to come they will know that a BAD MUTHAPHUCKKA named Sean X. Gunby Sr. lived and that his blood runs through their veins.

I AIN'T GOT NO TIME FOR BULLSHIT

Sunday, March 28, 2021

We still winning. This Shit Don't Stop!! My MIAMI ENTREPRENEURSHIP CONFERENCE is going down in less than 2 weeks (13 days to be exact) and I'm excited. I can't wait to hit that stage and put on a great show for the people. I've put the entire event on by myself with very little help. I have needed financing from outside sources and raised the capital necessary to put the event on. The ticket sales haven't been what I expected but nonetheless we still gawn put the muthaphuckkin' event on and shine like The Sun.

The mindset is strong, determined, focused, energetic and aggressive. This is what we do. We don't wait around for things to be given to us we get up and go out and MAKE SHIT HAPPEN. We envision the life that we want and then GET UP AND GO CREATE IT. We let nothing get in our way, we maintain our SELF-CONFIDENCE, BELIEF IN OURSELVES and we destroy the competition.

Sunday, April 18, 2021

I am at a loss for words for how hurt and angry I am right now. The pain is DEEP and ever present and it doesn't let up. It continues moving forward straight into my heart, soul and very constitution of who I am. I CAN'T FUCKIN BELIEVE THIS SHIT!! Out of nowhere through no fault of my own I got blind-sided by some shit that never should have happened. But it has. It has. It has. And it's fucked up.

All I can do is keep going another day, another day, another day, another day and another day KNOWING THAT THERE IS ALWAYS A CALM AFTER THE STORM. Something good is going to come out of this. Some way, some how............this painful situation is going to benefit me..... I just can't see it right now..... It's too dark...

THEM DARK MOMENTS

Sean G

Monday, April 19, 2021

You have to respect, protect and defend your honor and dignity all the days of your life or it will destroy your self-esteem and confidence. What do I mean honor and dignity?

Your values, your conceit, your arrogance, your self-confidence, your reputation, your name, your presence, your legacy and so much more. You have to PROTECT and DEFEND this at all costs. It's not so much about what the outside world will say or judge its about what you say to yourself and how you feel. How you judge yourself and how you feel about yourself is of utmost importance and you CANNOT hide from the fact that you left a violation of your honor unchecked.

I'mma man first. I'mma man first. And with that being said there is certain shit that cannot be allowed to "slide" because of what may or may not happen. YOU HAVE TO PROTECT AND DEFEND. Your protection and defense will soothe your soul and calm your spirit. Your protection and defense straighten your back up, embolden your mind, excite your walk, strengthen your eyes and soul. It's a must that you defend and protect your HONOR.

Wednesday, April 21, 2021

You will get knocked down in life GUARANTEED without a doubt, but it's what you do when you get knocked down. Do you stay down? Or do you get up? Do you whine and cry? Or do you have a short memory, dismiss it and keep moving forward. The choice is absolutely yours. It will be hard and mentally challenging to pick up the rubble from the explosion that took place in your life but either you pick it up, clean it up and move on or you stay STUCK LIKE CHUCK crying about some shit you can't control no more.

THE CHOICE IS YOURS!

■■

On October 22, 2020 my mother (Georgia Gunby) passed away at the age of 77. She lived a long life. She raised me from a little boy to a grown man and always had my back no matter what. I was always her pride and joy and she would move mountains for me no matter what the cause. After my SUN, (Lil Sean) was born I was replaced as her pride and joy and he took over.

When she would call to speak to him she would say "Hey how you doin'? Where's my BOY BABY?". She had said enough to me and wanted to get to Lil Sean. (ha ha smile). They would talk on the phone every day and he would go spend 3 weeks every summer with her down south at her house. This was the highlight of her life. Lil Sean went down there last summer for 21 days and she took off from work for 21 days straight in order to be with him every day. I loved this when he would go down there because I wanted him to get that "southern experience" straight from his grandmother much the same way I did back in the 1970's and 80's.

He would be having so much fun down there that he would barely call me. She waited on him "hand and foot" all day every day. Whatever he wanted she bought him. Whatever he needed she got it for him. She even wanted him to go to school down there for 2020 – 2021 and he wanted to. Too funny. He was truly her best friend and vice versa.

I never had any regrets about my mother passing as I felt that we had did everything a mother and son could do. I was 51 Yrs when she passed so I totally saw her end coming near and fully understood when it happened. I was satisfied and ok. I was at peace mostly because of her and Lil Sean's relationship that I saw grow, develop and unfold over his 9 years of knowing her.

Everything is cool. GEORGIA GUNBY STILL ALIVE

Thursday, April 22, 2021

After the success of the MIAMI ENTREPRENEURSHIP CONFERENCE I've decided to do another one in Atlanta, Georgia. I made a lot of mistakes with the MIAMI event because I just didn't know what I was doing and it was my 1st time ever doing anything like that. I lost thousands of dollars on that event but I gained millions of dollars worth of knowledge as to how to put on an event of that magnitude.

Having made those mistakes was a good thing. They are lessons and instructions on "what to do" and "what not to do". I also learned "how to do it" from trial and error and on the job training. Sometimes this is the best way to learn. To learn this way is nerve racking and painful but when you are finished you are that much more "seasoned" as to how to do it.

I'm looking forward to this joint and I'm expecting a far bigger turnout that MIAMI. MIAMI I launched in the middle of the COVID situation and MIAMI got a lot of bad press 2 weeks leading up to my event and that cost me a lot of ticket sales. Nonetheless, I pushed forward and didn't really care about the money as much as I did about making sure the event took place. My whole brand, name and reputation was on the line and that was more important to me than the money. Money can't bring you reputation or a good name. But, a good name and reputation WILL bring you money. Yes Indeed. So that was pretty much all I was concerned about leading up to the event... JUST MAKE SURE YOU GET THIS SHIT DONE!! The rest will take care of itself.

The event was a success. I got much good feedback from the attendees, speakers and vendors. Everybody felt the event and really enjoyed themselves. One of my major areas of concern was the vendors that paid me $250 for a table to sell their goods. I was worried that there wouldn't be enough traffic for them to make their money back and they would come back to me complaining. I WAS SHOOK UP ABOUT THIS PART. Nevertheless, there was plenty of traffic and ALL THE VENDORS made money and personally thanked me for hosting the event. I know I will be able to re-sell them a table at the ATLANTA event because of MIAMI.

All of the speakers showed up and all of the speakers got paid which was another part that I was proud of myself about. I wanted to make sure EVERYONE GOT PAID irrespective of whether I made money or not.
This was key to my name, reputation and BRAND. I put this high on my list. Because all it takes is for one "fuck up" and your name, reputation and BRAND are destroyed forever and most times can't make it back. Like I said, even though I lost "financial money" on the MIAMI event, I made "millions" on it as far as my name and reputation go. This is a FACT.

I was so stressed out leading up to the conference man that I couldn't wait for that shit to be over. It was constant pressure for 3 months and I wanted some relief. After the event was over I went back to the hotel room, took my clothes off, took a shower and just laid in the bed and CHILLED man. Shit was the ultimate relief. I had done it. I completed what I had started. I did it.

Friday, April 30, 2021

I want to talk to my mother. I want to just listen to her voice. Let her ramble on and on and on and on and on about whatever she wants to. Shit that I used to cut the conversation short for when she was alive. Just one phone call.

I'm still suffering from the events surrounding her death concerning my family stealing all of her property, insurance policies, jewelry, cars, houses….. everything. I'm embarrassed by it. I'm humiliated. I'm hurt deeply. I'm wounded. I'm depressed. I'm furious. I'm angry. I'm determined. I'm ready for war. I want blood.

I'm frustrated because I can't retaliate. For me to retaliate is for me to give up on my life and Lil Sean's life. For me to get even (even thought The Sun, Moon & Stars would sanction it) would put me, Lil Sean and our lives in the balance of the "white mans law". This bothers me. They deserve to be dealt with. They have it coming to them and they deserve everything that comes to them. I and very familiar with KARMA and it's mathematical exactness but I want to be the one who brings "it back around". I can't though and its fucked up. It makes me look weak. It makes me think I am weak which makes me feel weak. The impression is that "they dissed me and got over on me" that "they didn't respect or fear me enough" to not do what they did so I need to show them that they miscalculated and make a poor choice that they will never forget. This is my dilemma. I am very bothered by this and I'm stuck spiritually and mentally. I am at odds with myself. I am at war with myself as to what I know should be done justifiably so and what is prudent in my real world life. I'm fucked up!

I haven't been able to shake it. It haunts me day and night. I go to sleep with it and I wake up with it. I want revenge. I will get my revenge. In this lifetime I will get my revenge.

&&&&&&&&&&&&&&&&&&&&&&&&&&&&&&&&&&&&&&&&&&&&&&&&&

I'm looking to put on another event in Atlanta in August if all goes well and I'm able to raise the money I need to help me pay for it. I'm working on this as I write this sentence. I continue to move forward with my life in spite of the circumstances and what I think for feel. I have to keep moving forward. I'm in a lot of pain yes but I still can't stay "stuck like Chuck" and be fucked up mentally paralyzed. I have to push through this knowing that I will get to the other side of this and there will be better dayz ahead for me.

I am healthy. I just got done doing a "7 Day Juice Fast" which I completed and felt great. Dropped 4lbs and still going about 80% juice per day eating just one meal. Still working out heavy and I look amazing for 52 years old. I don't even consider myself or my age because I am so competitive and feel that I can compete with anybody. I still get my good 7 hours sleep every night which allows me to be on top of my game "every day all day".

Lil Sean is doing good. Getting big and growing every day and I'm with him day for day watching him. It feels good..

I have a good life.

Sean G

Wednesday, May 12, 2021

I'm back on my game STRONG!! I've gotten a new sense of drive, energy and enthusiasm to keep killin' the competition. You ask who is the "competition"? It's every muthaphuckkin' human being on the planet. I must outperform everybody. I must be more prepared than everybody. I must be more spiritually fit than everybody. I must be more mentally tight than everybody. I must be sharper than everybody. I must be "right" and do "right" so that "right" things happen in my life without me even trying. I have to think better than everybody. I have to eat better than everybody. I have to rest better than everybody. I have to sleep better than everybody. And then get up tomorrow and do the SAME MUTHAPHUCKKIN' thing all over again.

I mustn't be disrespectful to anybody. I mustn't do harm to anybody (unless they phuck with me). I mustn't be anti-social to anybody. I mustn't be a phuckked up individual to anybody. But I must "beat them at the game of life". My psychological peace depends on it. My financial bank account depends on it. My soul depends on it. My mind depends on it. My thoughts depend on it. MY LIFE DEPENDS ON IT.

Everything is good. I feel good.

Thursday, May 20, 2021

I'm going to have to "give myself" the kind of life and lifestyle that I want. I'm going to have to create the life that I want to have. Ain't no sense in waiting around for some other place, person, thing or institution to provide it for me. It's futile to wait on that. Ain't nobody comin' to help me and I don't expect or need it. I GOT IT!!!

I got to do this for me and it's possible. I just got to "get to work" and put "my entire mind on it" and never let up until I arrive at my destination.

Friday, May 21, 2021

The more I am becoming super certain that we are masters of our destinies through our thoughts, words and actions. I stay on top of my thoughts because my thoughts are the origin of my feelings. I have to continually ask myself "Sean, why are you feeling this way?..... What's wrong Sean?"

And being HONEST with myself.......

I can arrive at the exact nature of what is fuckin' with me and what I'm allowing to fuck with me. Even the bad shit can only impact my life to the extent I allow it to impact my mind. When I let shit "rent space for FREE" in my head and go up there and play kickball in my mind......I'm FUCKED UP! It's only until I stop and ask myself the questions as to what's bothering me and why can I change my thoughts and therefore my feelings.

I have the power and I am in control of this.

Tuesday, May 25, 2021

Man, LET THAT GO...... LET IT GO.... it's over and done with and there is nuthin' you can do to change what has happened already....... "FOR NOW" you can't let it impact your dome because you have some things in front of you that need your undivided attention and you can't be distracted wit bullshit......... "FOR NOW" you have to let it go..... There will come a time when and where you will be able to address it..... just not now...

Take care of your business that's in front of you and put your whole mind on it and do it to the best of your ability. Keep putting yourself in a position to win. Don't let dat shit affect your self-perception....keep dat high and always maintain control of that.... What they think is unimportant.... Their thoughts, talk and perception of you is not your REALITY.

Sean G

Saturday, May 29, 2021

I have to look no further than the mirror to find the solutions to all of my issues (don't like to use the word problems). I am my biggest issue. I am the primary reason I am not where I should be. I am the source of all of my weaknesses that I refuse to remedy. I am my greatest hindrance. I am the culprit. I am guilty.

I can't even front no more on myself. This time reminds me of the first 2 weeks in Federal Prison where I looked around and had nobody else to blame but myself and for the 1st time ever in my life I knew I was the only one that could "fix me". I knew what was wrong and had been running from it my whole life but now I had nowhere to run. I had to stand and fight myself. I did and the "NEW" Sean G won. And HERE I AM.

I'm at a similar place right now in another area of my life and some changes need to be made and I'm going to make them. Good thing is is that I have a reference point of having already been successful at making these types of "inner life changes" and knowing that only good can come from them. That the subsequent benefits of positive change are always good.

I'm tired of feeling the way that I feel and the time is now to fix this once and for all.

Sunday, May 30, 2021

YOU THE REASON WHY

You the reason why it ain't got done yet. You the reason why ain't nuthin' else related to that situation done took shape yet. You the reason why ain't nobody movin' the way you need them to move. You the reason why you hate your current circumstance. You the reason why you depressed. You the reason why you focusin' on everybody else and what they doin' inwardly resenting them because you ain't doin' shit. You the reason why your life "STUCK LIKE CHUCK". You the reason why you keep livin' in the past. You the reason why you fear the future. You the reason why you resent the present. You the reason why you outta shape. You the reason why your self-esteem low. You the reason why you ain't got no SELF LOVE. You the reason why you ain't got no SELF CONFIDENCE. You the reason why YOU HAVE TURNED INTO YOUR BIGGEST ENEMY. You don't have to look no further than your bathroom mirror to find the problem and the solution.

Peace out ………………..Sean G

Wednesday, June 2, 2021

GITCHYO ASS UP AND GIT BIZZY!!!

Ain't no sense in sittin' around thinkin' about yesterday, last month, 8 months ago, last year, 4 years ago...... I mean we all do this right.... I do....You Do..... They do..... WE ALL DO.....

But the WINNERS think about it BUT STILL KEEP MOVIN' FORWARD. Ain't nuttin' you can do to change dat shit. It's done. You can accept it or you don't have to accept it.... BUTCHU STILL GOTTA KEEP MOVIN' FORWARD....... you can't stop. That's when we die.... when we stop...

You will see alot of people who are still alive physically but you can tell by their body language, strength or weakness in their eyes, tone of voice and words they speak that their spirit is on life support and they are barely makin' it. We are not them... We take the bumps, bruises, cuts, broken bones, mental scars and spiritual wounds and we KEEP MOVIN' FORWWARD.. We see "our vision"...... We ain't gawn let nobody keep us from reaching "our visions"..... We deserve "our vision".......

GITCHYO ASS UP AND GIT BIZZY!!!

Peace out

Sean G

YOU DEPRESSED.....SO WHAT.... EVERYBODY IS..

Good Morning..... You depressed..... he depressed.... she depressed....they depressed..... EVERYBODY depressed....

But dat shit don't matter.... Nobody cares that you depressed or how you feel... They don't... You are the only one who cares and you are the only one who can "gitchu up outta" dat shit. You have to "gitchu up outta" dat depression. You can't stay there... YOU CAN'T STAY THERE..... Ask yaSELF honestly "what is wrong Sean?".... "What's the matter Sean?".... and HONESTLY tell yaSELF the truth as to why you feel the way you feel and what exactly is bothering you. Once you do this you are on your way to "gittin' up outta" dat shit and healing yourself.

There is no shame in being depressed. Don't let these fake ass TV, Actors, Entertainers, Instagram, YouTube, Athletes, Rappers make you believe that because they are showing you "the good life" in a 4 minute video that the other 1,436 minutes of their day is the same way...... BULLSHIT!!! THEY LYIN'.....
EVERYBODY GETS PUNCHED IN THE MOUTH BY LIFE.......
GITCHYO ASS UP AND GET BACK IN THE GAME!!
and always remember..

NOBODY CARES!

Sean G

THIS IS "YOUR LIFE".... NOT NOBODY ELSE'S

Man you better git real, know and truly understand that this "LIFE" you are living is "YOUR AND YOURS ONLY". Nobody else can live it for you. Nobody gave it to you. Nobody can fix it for you... This life was given to us by a power that nobody truly understands... Certain people profess to know what "LIFE" is and what it's all about but they guessin' too.....

You better go out here and live this thing man..... Ain't no comin' back once you gone. You outta here and within 2 weeks everyone has forgotten about you and moved on with the demands of their everyday lives. Not a bad thing it's just the way life is.

You have all types of opportunities, talents, gifts, ideas, imagination, visions and all that other fly shit muthaphuckkas be sayin'. Yes it's true but you have to MANIFEST THEM and ain't nobody gonna help you in the beginning. Dem Niggaz gonna show up when you dun made it.

Don't let nobody talk you outchyo game. Don't let nobody talk you outchyo dream. Don't let nobody talk you outchyo plan. If you believe in it and can see it in your mind..... THAT'S ALL THE PHUCKK YOU NEED....

Time to Git Bizzy

Sean G

IT GIT RUFF SOMETIMES.....

Yes it do..... Yes it do..... Without a doubt....... IT GIT ROUGH SOMETIMES man... I mean real rough to the point where you don't understand why and for what!! It seems like there is no let up in sight and things get bleeker, and bleeker and bleeker until the point you be like...... MAN GODDAM....HOW MUCH WORSE CAN IT GIT........ and it gits worse......
I understand that .... I've been there.......... It's not pleasant ...... Nor is it easy......
Butchu gotta hold on man..... You gotta just keep pushin' with all those thoughts and feelings understanding and knowing that "I'MMA GIT THROUGH THIS SHIT"...... "ONE DAY I'MMA BE ON THE OTHERSIDE OF THIS SHIT".... Just keep telling yourself that and you will speak it into existence... Examine your thoughts, perceptions, expectations and perspectives and ask yourself are they rooted in REALITY or BULLSHIT..... Once you determine this

then you gotta "CHANGE YOUR THOUGHTS" to something on a higher level, more positive and thoughts that make you feel better..... Rember the THOUGHT is the seed..... the FEELING is the fruit...... So you can best believe that however you are FEELING is directly tied to your THINKING....

IT GITS RUFF SOMETIMES................ BUTCHU YOU CAN SMOOTH DAT SHIT OUT!!

Sean G

Tuesday, June 15, 2021

DON'T WORRY BOUT DAT!! -- THAT AIN'T NUTHIN'.... KEEP MOVIN'

Man... Don't worry bout dat..... Tha's ova with... It done happened already and ain't nuttin' you can do to change what happened except your perspective of it... Look at the "reality" of it .... be real about it.... examine it.... then let dat shit go and KEEP MOVIN'.... Ain't no sense in keep rehashing that shit day after day after day after day..... It's done... Dat shit happens to everybody at some point in their lives..... You ain't by yourself.... Don't feel embarrassed or ashamed.....

ANOTHER LESSON LEARNED....

Sean G

Monday, June 21, 2021

PICK THAT PAIN UP....PUT IT IN Ya POCKET AND KEEP MOVIN' FORWARD

Yeah I know.... Yeah I know it hurt.... But that shit don't matter and don't nobody care. You gawn have to "pick dat pain up..... put it in ya pocket and keep movin' forward".... and guess what.... YOU CAN DO IT.... YOU HAVE TO DO IT ... because ain't nobody comin' to help you.
You ain't the only one going through a painful situation right now and this ain't gonna be your last one. This shit come and go... Ebb and flow..... To and frow... That's aight..... WE GOT IT..... WE CAN

HANDLE IT.... WE GAWN MAKE IT..... WE GAWN USE IT TO PROPEL US TO HIGHER LEVELS.....
Pick that pain up .... put it in ya pocket and keep movin' foward....

Friday, June 25, 2021

GIT UP OFF THE MAT!!!

You got knocked down...... SO WHAT!!! DON'T NOBODY CARE!!! GITCHYO ASS UP and check back into the game and show these Niggaz they can't phuckk witchu. Show them that "YOU GOT IT".... "YOU GOT IT"....   You ain't the only one that dun got knocked down... You ain't the only one that has taken a loss... You ain't the only one that dun got they heart broke.... You ain't the only one that dun lost all their money.... YOU AIN'T THE ONLY ONE..... Stop whinin' and cryin' ... don't nobody wanna hear dat shit....

Now GITCHYO ASS UP and check back into the game and go win the MVP trophy.

"I GOT IT".........

Sean G

Friday, July 2, 2021

TAKING ADVANTAGE OF OPPORTUNITY

When it presents itself you have to grab it... You have to take it.. It may never come back again. You may not get another chance so when it comes ... MAKE IT HAPPEN... It comes and goes all the time. I have missed many of opportunities in my lifetime when I was more fearful and less skilled at living. I've missed them in all areas of my life from business to relationships to you name it. And one thing I learned most importantly is that when OPPORTUNITY presents itself you have to take it.
I've taken advantage of alotta opportunities in my life that have changed my life for the better in all areas of my life. Now that I'm more experienced at living and more confident I don't miss many opportunties when they show up. I GRAB THEM...
Opportunity is a jealous woman and if you don't pay attention to her...... She will leave you.

THE 1ST DAY AFTER YOUR DEATH.... WHAT WILL YOU SAY TO YOURSELF?

On your 1st day after your death will you be satisfied with your performance here on Earth? Will you be able to sit back and chill and say "Man I KILT DAT SHIT".... "I DESTROYED DAT SHIT"... "I DID MY MUTHAPHUCKKIN' THING".... "I HAD FUN LIKE A MUUHHHPHUCKKA".....

Will you? Or will you have a bunch of regrets when you find out that nobody cared anyway and that you spend 20 – 40 years overly concerned with what others thought aboutchu.. That you lived in fear of being judged because you wanted the acceptance of others more than you wanted your own acceptance. That you were scared to take risks and chances that could've improved your life will you were hear on Earth. That you allowed other people who were "less than" you to influence you and hold forth over your mind. That you had all these gifts and talents that went to waste cause you was scared to be you. That you lived a life unfulfilled because you were afraid to be yourself which impacted your SELF-CONFIDENCE to the downside and obliterated your SELF-PERCEPTION and made your SELF-ESTEEM go out the back door and you lived your full life punching below your potential.

You better start asking yourself these muthaphuckkin' questions and taking a real close look at yourself and GIT BIZZY livin'.....

Sean G

I'm working through my pain. I'm suffering from day-to-day but nonetheless I keep moving forward. Sometimes I'm full of anger, other times I'm full of hurt, then I'm confused and upset. I struggle with what to do and what is the best course of action for me to take.

I look at my entire life in its reality and move accordingly even when it doesn't feel good. I've come a long ways. I have accomplished a lot in a short amount of time and my future is bright. Yes all of this is true....yet ..... I still think and feel "less than" my capability being that I've prevented myself from moving in the proper direction. This is temporary though. I will move forward with the "RIGHT" actions at the "RIGHT" time. Now is not the time. I remain strong.

++

I give myself time and I remain patient. Something BIG is going to happen for me real soon. I can feel it. I continue to remain diligent, focused, determined and full of faith that my hard work will pay off. I am in the best shape of my life right now all the way around. SPIRITUALLY, MENTALLY, PHYSICALLY. I am my strongest ever. I feel undefeated and unconquerable. I am capable of doing anything I wish. Yes I am. I am bound by nothing. I can rise above anything and prevail. I am success. Success pursues me.

My mental attitude is one of "no bullshit" no matter from who. I am not into buffoonery and fuckin' around wasting time. That ain't my thing... TIME IS OF THE ESSENCE and all of my seconds, minutes and hours will be utilized to the fullest. My heart is strong. My will is unshakeable. My mind is impenetrable and impervious to external influence. I stay tough.

Thursday, July 8, 2021

SPEAK UP!! SAY IT!! LET IT BE KNOWN!! BE SCARED.... BUT DO IT ANYWAY!!

At very important moments in my life when I should've spoke up I didn't and got what I deserved. If I would've just mustered up the courage and spoke up things could've and most likely would've turned out differently and most likely in my favor. I was scared at the time. I was afraid to say it. I didn't have the SELF-LOVE that would've pushed me to do it. My SELF-ESTEEM was in the basement and I convinced myself that I was unworthy. My SELF-CONFIDENCE was nonexistent so therefore I remained quiet and got what they thought I should have.

When I was a child this wasn't my fault as I wasn't trained up to speak up or taught "how to" speak up. However, when I became an adult and full grown man and I didn't SAY IT or SPEAK UP........then THAT WAS MY FAULT. Because I know better. Why would anyone bend to your position or make things happen in your favor if you don't STAND UP and SPEAK UP. Why would they? The human family is no inclined to do this. The human family is nothing more than "the most evolved form of animal" with the self-same instincts as an animal in the jungle. We only respect force, pushing, fighting (mental or physical) and confrontation. These are facts.

This is why I have to SPEAK UP for me. This is why I have to STAND UP for me. This is why I have to SAY IT and LET IT BE KNOWN. Because if I don't nobody will do it for me. It's my job and my responsibility to do that for the edification of my life. It's for the improvement of my existence. It boosts my SELF-PERCEPTION when I SPEAK UP FOR ME. It strengthens my SELF-ESTEEM when I let it be known irrespective of who it is. It builds my SELF-CONFIDENCE when I SAY IT and SPEAK UP FOR ME. This is very important to my life. It's either speak up and be SELF-RESPECTED or say nothing and suffer SELF-HATRED. The choice is mine.

For you is who I speak to, be afraid…..be nervous……be terrified but SPEAK UP anyway……you will get the courage, bravery and SELF-SECURITY after you do. You can't continue to live your life expecting things to happen in your favor and you ain't sayin' nuthin'… It don't work that way. You have to SPEAK UP! This makes all the difference in the world… For how would they know how you feel if you don't tell them? How would they know your position if you don't express it?

SPEAK UP!!! LET IT BE KNOWN!!

Friday, July 9, 2021

My future is bright. My best days are still in front of me. I've prepared for everything that is happening right now so nothing is impossible. We experience different challenges in our lives in order that we may grow, learn and become better at living and better people. Sometimes I forget that the rough parts are necessary and also part of the journey and are just as important as the times when we reach our goals. I miss that lesson sometimes and I begin to think and feel that the rough times are curse and meant to defeat me and prevent me from reaching my vision. But then I keep living and it is later re-revealed to me that the rough times are a necessary evil that provide the most growth opportunities.

The main thing is to keep believing, keep moving forward and stay cool knowing that the rain and sun work in tandem to make fruits

and vegetation grow. Nothing will grow without the other one.
They work together.

What is the meaning of life? What is the meaning of life inside of a
capitalistic society? What is the meaning of life in rural Central
America? What is the meaning of life in underdeveloped Eastern
Europe? What is the meaning of life in the major cities of China?
What is the meaning of life in the many different societies in
Africa?

WHAT IS THE MEANING OF LIFE?

I have no idea. I wish I had the answer for you "cut and dry" but I
don't. From my vantage point, there really is no meaning of life
other than SELF-PRESERVATION and to survive at all costs. To
make sure that I'm ok and Lil Sean is ok. Nothing more. It
sounds crude and insensitive but think about it. Think about your
life? Look at it. What are we doing here? What is going on?

If you asked this question to some of the different people in some
of the aforementioned continents and countries, all of the
responses would bare stark differences as they should. Because
our current circumstances affect and impact our immediate
thoughts and perceptions about our reality.

Why is it that certain people in certain places of the world were
born into "less developed" or "more developed" circumstances?
Why? Is it the "luck of the draw" where you are born? In which
country? And this having a major and material impact on your
existence here on Earth in this life.

The only certainty that I know is:

We are born and we are going to die and never come back.

I AIN'T PLAYIN' WICHY'ALL!!

I'M ON TOP OF MY GAME. I'M ON TOP OF DIS SHIT!! I'M GOIN'
HARD IN THE MUTHAPHUCKKIN' PAINT!! I GOT TO GIT TO MY
GOAL!! I AIN'T FINNA LETCHU NIGGAZ STOP ME FROM GITTIN'
MINEZ!! I KNOW YOU AIN'T GOT NO DREAMS. I KNOW YOU

AIN'T GOT NO AMBITION. I SEE YOU AIN'T GOT NO DESIRES. I SEE YOU CONTENT WITH MEDIOCRITY.. THAT'S WHY I STAY THE PHUCKK AWAY FROM YOU. YOU A WASTE OF MY MUTHAPHUCKKIN' TIME. I GOT TO GO!

I KNOW ALL TOO WELL THAT **"TIME IS OF THE ESSENCE"** AND I DUN ALREADY PHUCKKED UP AND WASTED ALOTTA MY TIME ON BULLSHIT IN MY PAST WHEN I WAS "YOUNG & DUMB". I AIN'T YOUNG AND DUMB NO MORE SO NOW I KNOW BETTER AND WHEN YOU KNOW BETTER YOU DO BETTER.

I AIN'T GAWN LIVE BUT ONE TIME. AND THEN IT'S OVER AND THAT'S IT. NOBODY CARES WHEN YOU ARE ALIVE AND DEFINTELY NOT WHEN YOU DEAD. THAT'S WHY I HAVE TO CARE. I HAVE TO GIVE A FUCK. I HAVE TO BE CONCERNED ABOUT ME. I HAVE TO HAVE MY BEST INTERESTS AT HEART. AND I DO.

I'M HAVING FUN LIVIN' MY LIFE. I'M ENJOYIN' DIS SHIT. OVERCOMING OBSTACLES. FIGHTING AGAINST ADVERSITY. MAKING COMEBACKS. ACCOMPLISHING SHIT. THAT'S WHAT THE PHUCKK I DO. I ACHIEVE!

SO I AIN'T GOT NO TIME TO BE PLAYIN' NO SILLY ASS GAMES. LIES. DECEPTION. MANIPULATION. MASK WEARING. FAKIN'. FRONTIN'......... MISS ME WIT ALL DIS SHIT.. GO FIND ANOTHER FAKE MUTHAPHUCKKA LIKE YaSELF TO PLAY DEM GAMES WIT. I AIN'T THE ONE. GIT THE PHUCKK OUTTA HERE WIT DAT SHIT. I'M TOO NICE WIT MINEZ TO LETCHU PHUCKK ME UP WIT DAT BULLSHIT.....

GIT DA PHUCKK OUTTA HERE WIT DAT BULLSHIT!!

Sean G

Tuesday, July 13, 2021

The one that can endure, persevere and stay committed is the one who makes it every time. In today's world (2021) this is what separates "those who do" from "those who don't". Nothing more. It's a mental attitude of tenacity and concentration. Everyone is dealing with something in their respective lives. Everyone has deep seated issues exclusive to themselves that causes pain, heartache, fear, confusion and panic. EVERYONE!

But it is those people who better manage these crisis situations and remain poised and steadfast in their pursuit of a brighter day. These people are able to "block out the bullshit" and penetrate to the core of a matter in a way that enables them to rise above trivial bullshit and get going with the business.

This is a must.

Thursday, July 15, 2021

I continue to do the things I need to do even though the progress is not moving as fast as I want it to. I get up and do the next right thing for the right reason and push my agenda forward. Sometimes I have a tendency to look around and judge myself, my platform and my consistency against others and I see them progressing but not me. But I quickly bring it back home and "look at the part I am playing" in my progress. The mistakes I'm making. The lessons I'm learning. The choices I'm making. And I have to conclude that I need to do better and focus more on what is working and get rid of that which is not working.

Often times I have to "slow my mind down" and enjoy the journey and understand that all of it is part of the dream. The good times, the bad times, the highs, the lows, the in betweens and everything else is necessary in order to win. It's about seeing it through until the end. That is the key.

■■

IMPATIENCE

One of my great enemies throughout my life that is constantly boring from within me. It's better than it used to be and I can "visibly" see it now as I've grown in more life experience and understanding. Yet it still remains always ready to knock me upside my head.

Sometimes "opportunity" gives me a bigger kiss when I am less impatient and allow things to just be and develop on their own. When I chill back and not try to force situations to ripen before their time I almost always get better results. I am still learning.

Friday, July 16, 2021

I've suffered some "self-manufactured" setbacks here recently at my own hands. Shit is phuckked up and I feel stupid. But I know I am learning from this. I know definitely that this will strengthen my will, augment my resolve and sharpen my focus.

The accomplishment ain't just when you get to the "top of the mountain" it's when you goin' up the mountain and all the shit you go through to get to the top. The slips, the falls, the scrapes, the cuts, the bruises, the twisting your ankle, the cutting your hands on the sharp rocks, the scraping your knees on the jagged edges, the running low on food and water, the hot sun beamin' down on your head draining you of energy and giving you Vitamin D at the same time re-energizing you. ALL THIS SHIT MATTERS. THIS IS THE MOST IMPORTANT PART OF THE JOURNEY.

Yet I still got up this morning, drank my coffee and GOT BIZZY destroying the competition all over again. My #1 competitor and enemy combined is myself.

I will win.

Sean G

Monday, July 19, 2021

We good. I GOT IT!! I'm regrouping and re-examining everything in my life at the age of 52. Yeap.. Yes I am.. It's much needed. I need to do this to carry myself upwards from the success that I've already achieved. Some things about me need fine tuning. In some areas my knives have gotten dull. Others need to be changed. And some areas flat out need to be thrown away and I need to start all over again re-building them back up.

I'm cool. CHANGE IS GOOD. I am going to separate myself from the "mediocrity" pack and blaze my own trail alone. I will achieve my goals and get to my destination before I die.

Friday, July 23, 2021

The "internal work" is the most important work of them all as it regulates the thoughts and the subsequent emotion that immediately follows. Self-regulation of what you allow yourself, your mind, body and soul to be exposed to is super important as this will dictate your life. I have to catch myself all the time and "dig" what I'm doing and determine if this is beneficial to me. Does it "add on" to my life? Does this move me forward to where I want to go? What is the point of this? These are some of the questions that I have to ask myself at times to make sure I stay on track.

Other than that I take it "one day at a time" and just continue to do my thing.

■■

What's real? What's fake? Who knows? I don't know. A lotta talk going around about this and that and what needs to be done and what is happening. I have no idea. I don't focus on that part. I hear it. I listen to it. But at the end of the day I really don't know.

What I do know is that I have to remain "REAL" with myself and my life. I have to remain "REAL" with my circumstances and the people that are in my life. I don't stay "REAL" with them for their sake but for my own psychology to make sure I'm keeping my finger on the pulse of MY OWN REALITY. Because someone is lying to me doesn't compel me to joint them and I start telling lies too. No I stay "REAL" and true to me so I don't fuck my head up. If they want to wear a mask and try to get over on me…….COOL….. That don't mean that I put on a mask too and engage in the bullshit with them. No. Truth is stronger than lies. REAL is stronger than FAKE. TRUE is stronger than FALSE. So in the end as long as I stay "REAL" I will preserve myself and come out on top for sure.

Saturday, July 24, 2021

STAY THE COURSE

There is alot of information, messages and sound bites telling us to do this…..do that…. don't do this…….don't do that……you shouldn't have done this…….you should do that…… It's important to stay the course and stay true to ourselves. Nobody knows definitively how this is going to end up… NOBODY…
But what I do know is that I have to stay true to myself so that I can love myself and live with myself. It's painful when you are in conflict with your spiritual and mental selves. There is no "peace of mind" there; only confusion, insecurity, worry, fear and unease. Not good.
Stay true to your course whatever that may be. You do not need to express, parade and convince anyone of your course…… ONLY YOURSELF! ………………….Sean G

Thursday,July 29, 2021

ALL I GOTTA DO IS SLOW DOWN AND TAKE MY TIME

I have a tendency to want to hurry things along and rush the process, forgetting that things take time to come together. That anything rushed usually doesn't end well. It's my mind. I have to slow my mind down and be learn to be satisfied with the "small inches" of progress that I make each day knowing that all those inches will eventually turn into miles as long as I remain consistent and keep doin' what I'm doin'.

Man, all I gotta do is "take my time" and be patient. It's a marathon and the race will go to him that can endure the long journey. He who has the mental stamina, fortitude and toughness to keep pushin' forward inspite of the obstacles, challenges, setbacks and failures. He who can pick himself back up again after being knocked down for the 43rd time. He who can find it within himself to get up and try again. She who will look at the positives in every negative situation and see the glass as "half full instead of half empty". She who can find reasons to persevere through the darkness and renew her inner fight and "try that shit again".

There is a way for you to make it. Without a doubt and without question it is there. It may be hidden or right in front of your face and you just may need to change your perceptions and perspective in order to discover it.

Or

You may have to create it from scratch. Use your ingenuity. Use your past mistakes. Use them past failures. Draw upon them past successes and remember that YOU HAVE DONE IT BEFORE AND YOU CAN DO IT AGAIN.

You have to find it.

These are the people who win.

∧∧

TWEAK, ADJUST & SOMETIMES REINVENT YOUR PROCESS

There are times where even though you are on the right track and making forward moves toward your envisioned destination, you will still need to re-examine your position and process (the moves you are making) in order to elevate higher and make sure you hit your mark. The examination of yourself is continual and often so that our knives are always sharp and can cut easily. IT NEVER STOPS.

I am at a point now where YouTube has "boxed in" my Channel where my views are continually dropping every single day even though I am uploading more and more videos. They are calling it "shadow banned". I have been stuck at 80,500 SUBSCRIBERS for weeks now with both my Revenue and Views falling.

At first it bothered me because I know my content is top-notch and deserves more views, however, with the political agenda, ideology and propaganda being pumped and rammed down the worlds mindset, if you are in any way on the opposite side of that then your social media progress will be restrained and/or stopped. I fully understand and accept that these huge technology companies are private entities and can do whatever they want as this is their right. I get it. However, as a MAN and knowing my true nature it was inevitable that I was going to have this issue given my rebellious nature and my propensity to speak out on issues that move me. So this I know was unavoidable for me and just a matter of time. It has hurt me financially in the short-term for sure but that's ok..

I've pivoted and started promoting more heavily and putting more emphasis on my PATREON CHANNEL which is a subscription based CHANNEL where my followers "pay a fee" to sign up and hear what I have to say. It's growing steadily and I'm encouraged. What's funny is that each time I sign up a new PATREON SUBSCRIBER it seems like my YouTube REVENUE falls the exact amount of the of new PATREON SUBSCRIBER PLEDGE. It's as if they are monitoring both pages at the same time to cap my money.

Doesn't matter to me because I'mma keep going. THIS SHIT DON'T STOP. My goal is to get 1,000 "consistently paying monthly PATREON SUBSCRIBERS" so that I can lock in that monthly revenue along with my T-shirts, books, hats, etc., both my other YouTube Channels (Sean G, THE PODCAST WITH SOUL), my mentorship sessions and my appearance fees for interviews and promotions. IT WILL ALL COME TOGETHER.

I've come along way from when I started this is 2018 and I never saw it morphing into what is has evolved in to. I NEVER SAW THIS COMING. This isn't what I projected nor did I even imagine the possibilities that have come as a result.

I get frustrated at times because I truly don't see anyone on my level as far as "carrying a message" is concerned. I see a lotta people with a lotta subscribers who are doing straight BAFOONERY and putting out garbage yet their channels are flourishing and growing and here I am pumping GOLD and my shit is shadow banned. Doesn't make sense. But I know deep down that the right person or people haven't heard me yet and when they do it will be a game changer and my life will never be the same. The recognition, critical acclaim, fame and money will be in abundance and I won't be able to stop it. Watch what I tell you.

In another sense I'm fortunate that it hasn't happened yet because when it does it will require extensive travel and huge demands on my time for about 2-3 years of which I'm ready to devote. In the meantime, I AM IN LIL SEAN'S LIFE FULLY. I am not removed from his life like so many other famous people are removed from their families and never get to "inject their SOULS" into their own children and the kids grow up never having spent time with their father and therefore don't really know their father. That is definitely not the case with me. My SUN knows his father intimately. For this I AM PROUD.

<u>**Friday, July 30, 2021**</u>

NO TIME TO WASTE

Get up! Let's go.... We ain't got no time to waste on yesterday...that shit is gone...over and done with. I gotta move on with MY LIFE. Nobody (no human) gave me this beautiful thing called LIFE...it came from a place and power that I don't fully understand. Nobody understands it even though they claim and profess to know.... BULL SHIT!! GIT DA PHUCKK OUTTA HERE.... You don't know just like I don't know....

But what I do know is that I am living today... right now in the "here and now" and that I am only here for a brief period of time so I must make the best of the cards that are in my hands. I can't re-shuffle the deck and get dealt a new hand. THIS IS WHAT I GOT and I go to play these muthaphuckkas. AND I AM.

I get up everyday in search of that brighter day. My pursuit of it is relentless. I fully understand that I am not after a particular destination that will bring me that brighter day but my brighter day is in the "here and now" ... this very day... this very moment. I have to see the good in everything even the PHUCKED UP PARTS as they are necessary for me to know what the DOPE PARTS are. The PHUCKED UP PARTS are whats makes me. The PHUCKED UP

PARTS are what solidifies me and fortifies my mind and soul and makes me unconquerable. The PHUCKED UP PARTS gives me my fight and my will to win. I NEED THEM.

For these reasons are why I am "up and at 'em" everyday with no hesitation because I fully understand that there is NO TIME TO WASTE

Sean G

UNJUST DISCRIMINATION

Not from a "race based" or "racial, creed, color or religion" perspective, which may apply to this talk, but from perspective even more trivial and stupid than that.

UNJUST DISCRIMINATION resulting from a differing of opinion or expression of an opposing viewpoint and as a result you are intentionally and deliberately "held back" and or "isolated" from your right to expression.

This is what I am currently going through as a result of my public support of Donald Trump as President and his policies as pertaining to world issues. I came out in support of him on my YouTube page and showed examples refuting what the mainstream media was alleging against him, and since that day my YouTube page has been "censored and shadow banned". My views have been cut resulting in reduced revenue to me, my subscribers have told me that they don't receive any of my "new video" notifications anymore and my subscriber count has been frozen for the past 11 months. It's fucked up how they are getting down. The written documentation supporting this country says that we have a right to the freedom of expression and a freedom of the press. Yet there is a open and notorious breach and/or violation of this basic right as far as The Constitution is concerned.

Allow me to clarify and add some more color to this…………..

Firstly, I fully understand that as a Black American that I am not covered by The Constitution nor protected by it since that at the time of it's crafting my people were "property, indentured servants or slaves" at the time. This is clearly spelled out in The Constitution.

Secondly, I understand that YouTube is a "private company", has it's own bylaws and policies and procedures, meaning that it can do whatever it wants, take any position for or against anything and push whatever agenda if chooses as it pertains to it business practices. I fully understand this. However, this all becomes blurred when YouTube, this same private entity, is "open and notorious" with it's "opposing support" of everything contrary to Donald Trump and even goes as far as to ally itself with very governmental powers that push the opposite agenda, effectively becoming a de facto quasi-governmental agency. SO FOUL.

This is where I take issue. YouTube is using it's substantial and massive power to push governmental agendas with bias. You can't be a "private entity" and at the same time aligning yourself with the government to silence, censor and isolate any opposing viewpoints. Now you are no longer protected by the "privacy" of your charter or bylaws, you are a governmental agency.

Now the question must be asked……….

Is America a democracy or a communist regime?

Sean G

$$

IT'S POSSIBLE

I'M UP THIS MORNING.. SLEPT GOOD. WENT TO SLEEP AT A DECENT HOUR. ATE CLEAN ALL DAY YESTERDAY. WORKED OUT YESTERDAY. SPENT TIME WITH LIL SEAN WATCHING THE MET GAME. SHOT SOME VIDEOS FOR MY YOUTUBE CHANNEL. GITTIN' READY TO PUT ON ANOTHER YOUNG BROTHER WANTING TO BECOME A YOUTUBER. HAD A PRODUCTIVE DAY ALL DAY WHICH IS WHAT IS DESIRED. THIS THING CALLED LIFE AIN'T NO BULLSHIT. THIS SHIT AIN'T NO GAME. YOU GOTTA SQUEEZE EVERTHING OUT OF THIS MUTHAPHUCKKA YOU CAN GET. AND IT'S POSSIBLE. YES IT IS… IT IS POSSIBLE… ABSOLUTELY IT IS POSSIBLE. BUT IT'S UP TO YOU TO BELIEVE DAT SHIT. AND THE DOPE SHIT ABOUT IS THAT YOU THE ONLY ONE THAT HAS TO BELIEVE IT. FUCK WHAT THEY SAY! FUCK WHAT THEY THINK! IT AIN'T UP TO THEM. IT'S UP TO YOU. AND ALL YOU HAVE TO SAY TO YOURSELF IS……..

IT'S POSSIBLE

I AM CAREFUL

I just keep moving forward in spite of whatever is happening around me. It really doesn't matter to me in that I am so focused and determined to see my vision through to completion that that is the only thing that I see. I am careful about my time. I am careful about my thoughts. I am careful about my conversations. I am careful about what I allow to enter my body. Whether through food, words, thoughts, music. EVERYTHING. I am careful.

I understand that most things have "life or death" in and of themselves as a standalone. Taken further, when I allow them to enter my mind, body or soul, then they definitely have life and I have to be careful how long I let them live or if I allow them to live altogether. Some thoughts must be killed immediately before they have a chance to permeate my mind and infect my dome with bullshit that leads me to nowhere or self-destruction.

It's a great time to be alive and be able to pursue my vision. That is a gift in and of itself. Just having the ability, chance and/or opportunity to wake up and go after what you imagined in your mind. That's freedom. That's life force. That's enthusiasm. Many people are not afforded this opportunity and are relegated to a life of doing something day in and day out that they don't want to do by their own volition but have to do it by force of their life circumstances. I am fortunate to have my life the way that it is. But don't get it confused. I built this shit like this. I designed my shit like this. I sculpted my life out of the pain, hurt, failures and setbacks to be what it is today. I envisioned this shit. I forced this shit. I made this shit. So it's my right to enjoy it.

■■■

THE PAIN, FAILURES & SETBACKS ARE NECESSARY EQUIPMENT

You need them. You need them. YES YOU DO!! But, Sean though this shit is painful man. This shit hurt man. I'm depressed man. I'm embarrassed man. I'm confused man.

YEAH I KNOW.. I BEEN THERE....

But you are right where you are supposed to be at the moment. The pain, hurt, setbacks and failures are CHARACTER BUILDERS. I know it don't seem like it but just keep living and you will see. We need these things to burn out the impurities in our souls. To get us RIGHT instead of always being fuckin' WRONG! This is a class better than any college course you can enroll in at any university in the world. THIS IS THE SCHOOL OF LIFE... and you are not alone and everyone has to matriculate through this class without fail. No matter who you are, where you live, where you from, your background, socio-economic status, who you know, who know you....none of that shit matters when it comes to the SCHOOL OF LIFE... You will take this course.

You can't "buddy-up" to the teacher and kiss their ass to get a good grade. You can't cheat on the quizzes and tests. You gotta pass every single assignment and hand in all of your homework. You will either pass or fail. No in between. Failing means DEATH..... Passing means LIFE.....

THE PAIN, FAILURES & SETBACKS ARE NECESSARY EQUIPMENT IN ORDER TO PASS THIS CLASS.

Sean G

Friday, August 6, 2021

TRUE or FALSE

If it comes from the heart then it's "TRUE" to the core. If it comes from the head then there could be some shit in the game and a greater chance for it to be "FALSE".

Why are we so afraid to be "TRUE"? Why are we conditioned to hide who we are by default? Is there really that much to loseby revealing who we really are? Is the potential for pain really that extraordinary and the pain so unbearable that I have to hide my "TRUE" to the core self?

I think not………

For what do I gain by concealing my "TRUE" and beautiful self? What are the benefits to this? Who am I protecting myself from? By being such, nobody never gets to truly meet me. Nobody ever gets the chance to know me. And if I am not careful I will fuck around and forget who I truly am

I don't understand the fake shit. At one time in my life I understood it because I was just that. I've outgrown that shit much to my benefit.

Saturday, August 7, 2021

CHANGE UP ON 'EM

Change up on 'em! Keep 'em off balance. Don't let them figure you out. Change your route. Don't answer the phone and see what they do and how they react. Show up at different places. Change your style. Change your conversation. Change your routine. Change your diet. Change your sleep hours. Change your morning routine. Change your thoughts. Change up your perspectives. Change from the inside out.

CHANGE UP ON 'EM

But always remain true to you!

Sean G

Made in the USA
Middletown, DE
05 September 2021